Curiosity

Curiosity

The secret ingredient for success in personal and professional growth

STEFAAN VAN HOOYDONK

CAPSTONE
A Wiley Brand

Registered Office
John Wiley & Sons Ltd, The Atrium, Southern Gate, Chichester, West Sussex, PO19 8SQ, UK

For details of our global editorial offices, customer services, and more information about Wiley products visit us at www.wiley.com.

Wiley also publishes its books in a variety of electronic formats and by print-on-demand. Some content that appears in standard print versions of this book may not be available in other formats.

Library of Congress Cataloging-in-Publication Data

Names: Hooydonk, Stefaan van, author.
Title: Curiosity: The secret ingredient for success in personal and professional growth/ Stefaan van Hooydonk.
Identifiers: LCCN 2024040473 (print) | LCCN 2024040474 (ebook) | ISBN 9780857089809 (paperback) | ISBN 9780857089823 (ebook) | ISBN 9780857089816 (epub)
Subjects: LCSH: Curiosity. | Success in business.
Classification: LCC BF323.C8 H66 2025 (print) | LCC BF323.C8 (ebook) | DDC 650.1—dc23/eng/20241114
LC record available at https://lccn.loc.gov/2024040473
LC ebook record available at https://lccn.loc.gov/2024040474

Cover Design: Wiley
Cover Images: © john/Adobe Stock Photos; © amedeoemaja/Adobe Stock Photos

Set in 13/16pt Sabon LT Std by Lumina Datamatics

SKY10093227_120624

Dedication

*I dedicate this book to you, the reader.
Simply because you empower yourself to rock your
world. You will find that the light shines brighter
on the other side of the status quo.*

Acknowledgements

Wow—where to start? First of all, I would like to say a huge thank you to all people who uplifted me during my entire life. Your big and small gestures of kindness made me the person I am today. Without you, I would be a lesser version of myself. Without you, this book would not be born.

Thank you so much to the growing group of fellows at the Curiosity Institute: Clare Inkster, Soren Meibom, Hilary Lichterman, Robert Danna, Laci Loew, and Alexandre Santille. Your energy, ideas, guidance, collaboration, and support mean the world for me. You help me grow. Thanks for your insights; they are nurturing the flame of curiosity throughout this book.

Thank you to all the leaders all around the world for inviting me to work with you. You are the early adopters of intentional curiosity. Thanks for your passion to baseline and benchmark curiosity in your departments and organization, to bring me in to inspire your (management) teams and to help them to activate curiosity. Your company cases, feedback and encouragement has given me purpose to go deep into the concept of curiosity. You will recognize them in this book.

This book would not be here without the incredibly rich conversations I've had with the wonderful people who graciously opened their schedules to be interviewed for the book. A big thank you to all those who allowed their stories and advice to be featured in this book, including Lynn Borton, Tasha Eurich, Steven Shepard, Yogesh Kumar, Jim Hamakiotis, Yury Boshyk, Rob Theunissen, Bilal Sununu, Marc Ramos, Cecile Cremer, Sharath Baburaj, Simon Brown, Teddy Frank, Luke Revell, Thom Crockett, René van Dormael, Mike Pino, and Claire Bown. This book is even more valuable and relatable because of your contributions.

I am grateful for the collaboration with the team at Wiley for all their help and support. This is my second book, and the team has always been on hand to support. Big thanks to Annie Knight, who encouraged me to write this book, Alice Hadaway to ensure smooth sailing through the process from idea to printing and Tom Dinse to review and provide guidance in the first manuscript.

Thank you so much to my parents, they introduced the path of curiosity to me early on. I remember this one time when they kept me out of school so they could take me to a Tutanchamun exhibition. I must have been 8 years old. Defiant acts like these showed me that permission for bending the rules to explore something new and meaningful is ok.

To my partner Jeltje Peletier, thank you for supporting me in every crazy thing I do (like write another book or invest in agricultural land to start a foodforest). You have the ability to get the best out of me with your gentle touch. You know when to give me space or when to lean in. You are the best friend I could wish for. I'm looking forward to writing our next chapter.

Finally, this book is for my children: Rik, Femke, Koen, and Menko. As you are getting launched in professional life, I am more and more convinced that "things" big and small must be done differently. We have come out of a twentieth century which created the mess we are currently in. The twenty-first century is different and requires new tools. Curiosity is probably the most important one of them. I am grateful that you have plenty of it, each in your own special way. The world is safe in the hands of people like you. I hope this book can provide some extra ideas.

About the Author

Stefaan van Hooydonk is founder of the Global Curiosity Institute and bestselling author of his first book: *The Workplace Curiosity Manifesto*. An experienced global C-suite executive, Stefaan held executive roles as Chief Learning Officer in Fortune 200 companies like Royal Philips, Cognizant, Saudi Aramco, Nokia and others. He consults global corporations and leadership teams towards building a stronger curiosity muscle. Stefaan researches the topic of workplace curiosity in companies. He believes that curious individuals need curious environments to thrive and that especially in times of turmoil individuals and companies need to embrace intentional curiosity. With the help of unique diagnostics, he creates insights on what drives and what enables individuals and organizations to show up curiously. He is a regular speaker around the world on the power of curiosity to benefit professionals, leaders, teams, and organizations.

Contents

Introduction

Trigger Question: do you consider yourself a curious professional?

In the present business landscape, the idea that curiosity is one of the key defining factors of success is popular and even obvious.

- The headhunting company Egon Zehnder has settled on the concept of curiosity as the biggest predictor of executive success.
- The World Economic Forum places curiosity in the top skills next to skills like analytical thinking, creativity, and agility.[1]
- Internal research by LinkedIn has found that there is a 90% growth in the use of the word "curiosity" in online job ads. If you want to recruit the best talent, use curiosity in your recruitment communication. Curiosity sells.
- Leaders often consider themselves as having a great deal of curiosity, and more than the people around them. After all, their track record is better than others in sticking their neck out and exploring new possibilities.

Not so fast.

At the beginning (of relationships, start-ups, new projects) we are often open and humble, only to find ourselves sliding into a state where we stop asking important questions. We stop exploring. Over time, we settle for the status quo. When we find ourselves for too long in the same role, we don't play to win anymore, we play-not-to-lose and hold on to the past.

Though curiosity is socially desirable, and many people associate themselves with being curious, most of us are more drawn to its opposite: conformity. We say we are curious, yet we often are quick to cast judgement on others rather than engage with curiosity, we comply with societal norms of what constitutes success rather than defining our own norms. For better or for worse, we as a species have a genius for getting used to things, especially when things are gradual and incremental.

It is impossible to calculate the wasted time and resources created by a conformist mindset. Phrases like "I/we always do it this way", or "This is the way the company wants us to do things" prevents innovation from happening. It is just as hard to measure the emotional toll. Most of us go out of our way to remain conformist and not stick out our necks, denying ourselves new adventures, innovation, and small and large growth opportunities.

This book is about the magic curiosity can bring to our lives, teams, and organizations if we focus on it with intent. If we let it. We'll explore together the three important prerequisites for curiosity to flourish: permission, awareness, and intentionality. Without them, curiosity diminishes over time.

We will also discuss the fact that curiosity is more complex than we often think. For instance, curiosity is more than a mere intellectual pursuit into the unknown. Curiosity is also about keeping our relationships healthy. Equally, curiosity helps us to go inwards and question our inner state of mind.

In this book, we will explore what makes curiosity so difficult to put into practice and maintain over time in our day-to-day lives and in the institutions we build.

It is also about how we can do better.

I not only study workplace curiosity for a living, I am also a recovering conformist. Though people say that I am a curious individual and professional, I am the first to say that I am a curiosity work-in-progress case. When faced with stress, I don't take time to listen. When things go wrong, I try to blame others. When a lucrative project coincides with a planned holiday, I lean towards postponing the time off with my family. When I think I am not good at something, I put it off. The list goes on and on. To come to terms with my shortcomings, and to help you to do the same, I decided to research the power of curiosity.

Nearly everyone thinks or believes that curiosity is an individual trait, and in fact many people pride themselves that they are above average when it comes to curiosity. Indeed, curiosity—the intentional and self-aware variant—benefits the individual in many ways.

Based on my research and work with many professionals and organizations over the years, I have come to believe something counterintuitive: the real power of curiosity lies in its collective power. If we start supporting curiosity in our people and make it a collective trait of our organizations, we will create organizations that not only thrive in the present, but also future-proof themselves.

This book introduces an important new idea for all companies:

Make curiosity the organizing principle of management thinking and action.

In today's environment of near constant revolution, a singular focus on the status quo risks implosion. The management consultant Gary Hamel has it right when he says: "Obedience, competence and diligence are commodities. Passion, initiative, creativity and curiosity is what companies need (and short in supply)."[2]

Only the curious companies, and managers, can find their way to the future.

I came to be interested in the power of workplace curiosity when I was responsible for a large transformation project for a global IT services company of 300,000 employees. I was the Chief Learning Officer. The company had been growing through global regional expansion. For every new customer, new resources were recruited. Given the rapid expansion of the company, rotating people across customers was part of the process. This approach had been a successful strategy when specialized resources (in Artificial Intelligence (AI), the Internet of Things (IoT), Machine Learning (ML)) were not readily available in the market, but required a radical change for the company—to also encourage the existing employees to upskill themselves and to actively support job mobility.

This new approach to balance hiring new employees with upskilling the existing workforce set in motion many changes. For instance, customer contracts needed to be renegotiated to allow for more workforce flexibility. Managers needed to allow for internal rotation of their best resources.

The biggest change, however, was in the learning and development of the 300,000 employees around the world. Not only did they need to keep their existing skills current (not an easy thing in the fast-moving world of IT), they also needed to think about what new job they aspired to and reskill themselves accordingly. The role of the learning and development department was to orchestrate and enable and also to communicate a new strategy and a new deal: namely that we were going to push fewer courses and less content, but empower every colleague to decide for themselves what new skills they fancied.

This new strategy was supported by the board and the CEO was glad to kick off the project. The initial response from the employees to our internal marketing efforts was excellent. Then it plateaued. A minority jumped at the opportunity of acquiring highly in-demand skills. The majority could not be bothered. Or so it seemed. Even though senior management gave permission, many employees had lost some of their childhood ability to tap into their curiosity.

Many leaders also lacked the skills to create curious workspaces. Realizing this, we trained people in the concept of curiosity. In online sessions, we trained people on the concept of neuroplasticity (aka your brain is agile and you can change, regardless of age), shared with them how to think about curiosity, what it is, how it works, and also what its barriers are. Checking in with people three months after the session with a simple survey inquiring how the concepts of the curiosity session still resonated, the majority indicated an increase in their desire to embrace novelty. This felt already good. The real insight came when we compared the training people who had followed the curiosity session with those who had not over a 12-month period after the session. What we found was that those who were exposed to the curiosity session had consumed twice as much training compared to colleagues who had not.

This pilot provided an important lesson: permission is the necessary starting point. Providing tools for people to change their behaviour comes second. Changing culture comes third.

After this project and training more than 15,000 people in the company, I left my cushy corporate job and set up the Curiosity Institute. I wanted to dive deeper into the concept of curiosity, especially how and why it influences individual and corporate success. I researched its complex nature and created tools to measure curiosity in individuals, and also in teams and organizations. I wrote a first bestselling book in 2021: *The Workplace Curiosity Manifesto*.

It was the beginning of the COVID-19 crisis, so not an ideal time, you might think, to set up a new venture. But that turned out to be not really the case; things picked up really well. I have worked with 50-plus companies, have inspired more than 20,000 professionals with inspirational talks, have gathered data from over 10,000 professionals and 30 companies.

Why Curiosity, Why Now?

Since the dawn of time, humans have had a love–hate relationship with curiosity. On the one hand we celebrate people who stick out their necks and explore the world. The most obvious examples are our own children. They are born with an innate desire to learn. Curiosity enables them to make sense of the world, to learn how to interact with others, and learn about themselves.

On the other hand, curiosity also killed the cat. We frown upon people who ask difficult questions, who challenge the status quo. Most leaders demand obedience and conformity from their team. Even though they say they want to work with the best of the best, their actions often reveal that they prefer to lead people who are not challenging the status quo.

When I ask leaders whether curiosity is a good thing for an organization: 90% say yes. When I ask them whether they are inviting curiosity into their teams: only 52% agree. There is clearly a say/do gap. In theory they agree that curiosity is a good thing. In practice, they prefer that others are bold, not them. Saying something is not the same as doing it.

We allow individuals to be curious yet, when people form groups, we demand conformity. We embrace curiosity and at the same push it away as an unwelcome guest. Even the Bible frowns upon curiosity. Think about Eve trying to eat an apple from the tree of knowledge. We all know what happened.

I have dubbed the twenty-first century the "century of ideas". For corporates, the twentieth century was the century of relative status quo, one where scale and scope was needed to be successful. Let's compare two companies: the Marriott hotel group and Airbnb. Marriott took about 90 years to amass 700,000 beds in 90 countries. Airbnb reached the same scale in just four years—different philosophy and business model. If stock markets are an indication of value, Airbnb is 50% more valuable compared to Marriott.

The times when we could copy-and-paste last year's strategy as a guide for the current year are over. The past is at best an advisor, at worst a detractor. The efficiency mantra we learned in business schools is still useful, yet the fast new business realities require leaders to learn a new skill: the skill to combine operational excellence with a humble openness to the future.

In my first book I focused on the power of intentional curiosity for professionals. I found that curious professionals progressed faster in their careers and made more money than their less curious peers. Curious professionals learn faster and more deeply, are more ready to embrace change, and are better at forming and maintaining relationships. They are also more self-aware.

Individual curiosity has many benefits yet, as mentioned, its ultimate value lies in its collective power. COVID-19 has been a testament to the remarkable power of collaboration to battle crises. Individuals cannot solve a crisis, but communities can.

The more leaders and corporations create conducive platforms for new ideas and their implementation, the more solutions—big and small—will see the light of day. Hopefully, these solutions will benefit not only the company, but also the community and the planet.

Another reason is that curious professionals need curious teams and curious managers. Those curious professionals who are not supported by a curious culture will either burn out, become conformist cogs in the system, or simply leave for more curious companies.

About This Book

This book is for anyone who sees her or himself as a force for good. The book is written especially for those people who want to reshape their team and ultimately their organization into a better version of itself.

Every chapter is filled with stories, frameworks, and useful information to deepen your depth of knowledge of curiosity. You will find every chapter starts with a quote. I encourage you to read the quote, even say it out loud and reflect on it for a moment. The quote is followed by a trigger question: a question you are invited to answer for yourself. To make the concepts of each chapter stick, I have included questions for reflection at the end of each chapter.

The book offers frameworks that I hope will help you think about, talk about, and practise curiosity in a way that allows you and the people around you to work and live more joyfully.

The book is made up of four parts. The first part will dive into the neuroscience of (collective) curiosity: what we know about curiosity, what it does, how it works, and what its barriers are. The second part will outline a model anyone can use to maximize curiosity at the individual level, and also at the level of the collective. The third part will deepen some specific areas, such as the role of the leader, or culture, or artificial intelligence. I will also expand into some broader themes, such as the relationship between good citizenship and the planet. In the last and fourth part you will be offered a conclusion and a call to action.

Ready to dive in?

We'll start with the basics. Let's explore what curiosity is, what it does, how it works, and investigate why curiosity is key for individuals, teams, and organizations.

Let's do this.

Notes

1. https://www.weforum.org/agenda/2023/05/future-of-jobs-2023-skills
2. https://thehypertextual.com/2010/04/08/gary-hamels-pyramid-of-human-capabilities/

Part 1

The Why and the What of Curiosity

Curiosity is essential in today's rapidly changing world, driving innovation, learning, and adaptation by challenging the status quo and promoting continuous exploration and discovery. Given that the concept of curiosity has entered boardroom discussions, it is necessary to explore its meaning and implications at a deeper level. That's what we are doing in Part 1. We discuss what curiosity is, how it works, and what it does. Today, it enjoys a predominantly positive view but still faces challenges within rigid systems. Neuroscience teaches us that curiosity enhances learning and creativity by activating brain regions related to reward, executive control, and memory, triggering a craving for new information similar to hunger. Moderate stress enhances curiosity, while excessive stress inhibits it. Understanding and leveraging the neuroscience of curiosity enables individuals and organizations to foster environments that encourage continuous learning, innovation, and personal growth.

1

The Business Case
for Curiosity

"Open the window, it's a big world out there."
Sakichi Toyoda, founder of
Toyota Industries Corporation

"If you're comfortable, you're doing it wrong."
Ted Lasso, TV character

Trigger Question: overall, would you say that curiosity is encouraged at your company?

Envisage a world where we recognize that unknown unknowns are the primary catalysts of economic and social change. Unknown unknowns are things that we are neither aware of nor understand. In this world, everything is considered an "accident" in the statistical sense, with finite probabilities of occurrence. This shift means that familiarity can no longer be relied upon, and it has profound implications for expertise, know-how, assumptions, and predictions. Amidst ever-increasing organizational and contextual complexity, professionals collaborate, ploughing through vast knowledge and unprecedented data volumes, often assisted by machines.

This description of future work implies torrents of high-knowledge content and accelerating complexity, which some leaders are already experiencing as today's reality. An organization that lacks curiosity risks becoming complacent, failing to learn from mistakes, fostering arrogance, and missing out on innovation in the face of new competition. How well-suited are our present organizations and leadership styles for such a situation? That's the question this chapter will answer.

What Is Curiosity?

Curiosity is the mindset that challenges the status quo, driving discovery, exploration, and learning.

While curiosity is often associated with children exploring the world, it's equally crucial for adults, helping them to learn and grow, fostering positive connections between people and driving innovation for companies. Being curious means actively seeking novelty, welcoming ideas that challenge our viewpoints, and letting our mistakes trigger curiosity rather than embarrassment. It means asking, "Why was I wrong? What can I learn from it?"

Three dimensions of curiosity

We'll dive into the various components of curiosity in later chapters. For now, it suffices to introduce the dimensions of curiosity. Curiosity, as a concept, comprises three dimensions:

- Transpersonal Curiosity: This dimension is about the thirst for knowledge, the desire to explore the unknown, and the drive to understand the world around us. It motivates us to seek answers to questions and challenges the status quo. It can also be referred to as intellectual curiosity.
- Interpersonal Curiosity: This dimension relates to our interest in people, their stories, and their perspectives. It drives us to connect with others, build relationships, and

gain insight into different viewpoints. It can also be termed Empathic Curiosity.

- Intrapersonal Curiosity: In this dimension, curiosity turns inward. It involves self-reflection and a deep desire to understand our own thoughts, emotions, and motivations. It prompts us to question our beliefs and biases. You can also use the term Self-reflective Curiosity, if you wish.

The Importance of Curiosity for Organizations

Curiosity drives innovation, prevents settling for the status quo, nurtures organizational humility, and promotes divergent opinions. It supports organizational learning, particularly in the context of after-action reviews, and encourages learning from failures. Start-ups, unburdened by rigid routines, excel in this aspect, being four times more likely to learn from mistakes compared to mature organizations.

This does not mean that scale-up or grown-up companies are lost to curiosity. There are numerous examples of grown-up companies who challenge the status quo inside their organization and successfully embrace innovation in products and services and/or customer and employee engagement.

For instance, when comparing the global sub-scription numbers of on-demand television between the "new" Netflix and the "old" Disney, we see that the Disney+ has been overtaking Netflix for a while already. With the right focus, established organizations can also embrace curiosity and outpace start-ups.

In times of change, standing still means moving backwards. Leadership teams that embrace curiosity create thriving organizations, constantly improving their current operations and preparing for the future.

The Implications of Curiosity for Leaders

Curiosity requires champions. A manager's curiosity profile significantly influences their team's curiosity appetite. When a manager demonstrates a high propensity for curiosity by modelling it, generating ideas, questioning the status quo, and showing a hunger for learning, their team responds in kind with a high collective learning footprint.

Conversely, when a manager does not emphasize the importance of learning, the team becomes reluctant to consume knowledge or share their expertise. Role modelling also includes asking questions, actively listening in meetings, and being open to different answers.

Your answer to the trigger question at the beginning of this chapter ("Overall, would you say that curiosity is encouraged at your company?") will have a direct relationship to how well your leader is managing the team: whether they are uplifting the team towards openness and exploration or, on the other hand, stifling them.

The overall answer to the question varies per team. I encourage the leadership teams I work with to look for best practice teams and praise their leader's ability to create curiosity. Overall, however, 51% of employees report that their company encourages curiosity. The good thing is that half of employees feel empowered. The other half just needs to be invited onto the bus.

Additionally, if agility in volatile times is important, it pays for leaders to focus on how much their culture and operational processes support curiosity. For instance, whether employees feel that they can ask questions at work. My research has shown that 65% of employees feel they cannot.

The top four barriers to curiosity, as shared by employees and managers in my diagnostics, are, in this order:

1. Top-down decision-making by management.
2. I am too busy to explore new ideas.
3. We don't learn from our mistakes.
4. Inquisitiveness and creativity do not lead to public or financial recognition.

Understanding the status quo helps. Once we know it, we can do something about it.

Reverse Feedback

A good sign of a really curious leader is whether they ask for feedback from their team members. This is also called "reverse feedback" indicating that feedback can also flow from the subordinate to the manager instead of the other way around.

How often does your manager ask this simple question: "How am I doing as your superior?"

Such a simple, open question requires humility and vulnerability on the part of the leader. Humility to acknowledge that subordinates can give the manager important feedback. And vulnerability to ask the question in the first place.

Few managers ask this question. In surveying more than 30 global companies and thousands of professionals, I have found that only 23% of first-line managers, 46% of mid-level managers, and 6% of senior execs ask this very question.

According to self-awareness researcher Tasha Eurich, people prefer not to ask for feedback because it makes them uncomfortable. She distinguishes three kinds of excuses to justify not asking this question: She calls this the "Ostrich trinity".[1]

The first excuse is "I don't need to ask for feedback". This excuse is driven by arrogance where the person thinks they are superior and right and that the opinion of others does not matter. The second excuse for only a few people asking the question can be summarized as "I should not ask for feedback". Here there is a worry that asking the question negatively influences the relationship, as if asking the question conveys weakness or comes at a cost. The third kind is "I don't want to ask for feedback". In this case, the person dreads the potential answer and fears they might not like it.

The truth, however, is this: when we ask for feedback, something interesting and counterintuitive happens. Our relationships become better because people naturally reward us for seeking critical feedback. When we do so, we are also perceived as being more efficient (by bosses, peers, and employees); further, our humility gets rewarded with a new perspective on how we can improve.

The research is clear about the correlation of good versus bad leaders and how readily they ask for feedback: 83% of top-performing leaders regularly solicit feedback, compared to just 17% of the worst-performing leaders.[2]

Why Is Curiosity Hard for Professionals and Organizations?

Everyone is born with curiosity, but its object and degree vary based on individual circumstances. As we go through life, some of our curiosity becomes dormant. Similarly, companies and organizations can either grow or diminish their capacity for curiosity. The main reasons for diminished curiosity in both individuals and organizations include a mindset of thinking we know, the schooling system, fear, stress, routine, limiting beliefs, algorithms (as explained in Chapter 3), and non-conducive environments. A lack of curiosity prevents individuals, organizations, and societies from becoming their best versions.

Curious professionals are proactive, aiming to win, while incurious ones aim to avoid losing. In the era of the fourth industrial revolution, driven by information technology and biotechnology, companies cannot afford to be incurious. An organization that lacks curiosity will become complacent, fail to learn from mistakes, foster arrogance, and miss out on innovation in the face of new competition.

A Shift in Culture

For a century, management thinking rooted in perpetuating the past and command-and-control leadership has hindered curiosity's growth. This culture often promotes conformity over curiosity. However, with the right motivation and external support, we can rediscover our innate curiosity. The COVID-19 pandemic has brought radical change, and it's the curious who thrive, whether individuals, organizations, or societies. Remember that curiosity is intrinsic; we just need to reconnect with it.

A growing number of professionals and companies have embraced the curiosity movement. In these organizations, leadership teams recognize the power of curiosity. They grant permission, assess individual and organizational curiosity, establish curiosity Key Performance Indicators (KPIs), identify curiosity drivers and detractors, and integrate curiosity into corporate values and core processes, such as innovation and go-to-market strategies. Companies like Dell, Nike, ChampionX, Disney, NASA, Novartis, and others lead the way.

Curiosity is the engine of growth in our world. Especially when change is the only constant. Curiosity helps us to explore new possibilities and gets us out of our comfort zone. Curiosity drives us forward, generates new ideas, and helps us and the world around us to evolve. Curiosity helps us challenge the status quo. It moves us from entropy to evolution and enables us to continue to test, learn, experiment, and grow. It's also at the heart of business success with research suggesting it really is the secret ingredient to successful, happier, more creative, and more inclusive workplaces.

Imagine how different our world would be without curiosity. We would not be interested in news or reading articles; would not try to understand the effects of climate change; would not be keen to meet new people, design new products, and services for our companies, improve our environments; nor reflect on our own beliefs, travel, or collect stamps. Nor create better products. Nor start new companies.

The Opposite of Curiosity

As the founder of the Global Curiosity Institute, you might think I am a curious individual. In reality, I am a recovering conformist. I also often relapse into situations where my curiosity gives way to conformity.

Let me share a personal example to explain why conformist behaviour is often stronger than curiosity.

There is this Vietnamese restaurant close to our house in the old centre of Antwerp. We live right in the middle of the beautiful old town. I read recently that Antwerp was named the most idyllic place to visit in Europe. If you are into historic centres and interested in Belgium, I'd say that Bruges is the first place to visit, closely followed by Antwerp. When walking around the cobblestone streets, it is easy to imagine oneself back in time. My neighbour, who happens to be a city-guide, told me that Antwerp used to be bigger than London in the sixteenth century. With all that history, Antwerp is a magnet for intellectual curiosity. In 2022, 11.6 million visited this radiant city.[3]

With all these international visitors, there are lots of wonderful restaurants. Because we lived many years abroad, we are often drawn to international restaurants. When we just moved houses, we explored all of the restaurants in the immediate vicinity. Now, one year later, we find ourselves going back to the same restaurants we consider to be good.

This is one aspect of curiosity: it decreases over time. In the beginning we are high on exploration; after a while we settle into routines which feel good. These routines are woven into our lives. We take the same road to our favourite store, we tend to stick to our preferred channels of news, we eat lunch in the office with the same group of colleagues just because it feels good, it is easy, it does not require us to spend energy. We are on automatic pilot.

These routines make life easy for us. Without them, life would be much harder. I would hate to rethink every day where I would get my daily dose of news from, or what new recipe of baking bread I should try. Our Vietnamese restaurant is not very different. The atmosphere is good and cosy, the owners know us by now—that we like Jasmine tea and that I always ask for an extra portion of Basmati rice.

We also order the same dishes every time. There are two reasons for this: one rational and one emotional. The rational reason is that their vegan/vegetarian options are limited, so we kind of need to choose among a limited set of options. A more important reason is emotional: we know what to expect with each dish and gladly revisit our comfortable early choices.

During keynotes, I often ask people to indicate with a show of hands whether they like to go back to the same restaurants. You should see the response as many hands go up. Then I ask the group whether they then order the same familiar dishes they know to be good, or explore new dishes they have not tried before. Believe it or not: there are more people who reorder the same dish rather than explore new ones.

What is your normal go-to strategy in selecting a restaurant? Or where to order a take-away? Or what to cook tonight?

If you find yourself going to the same place, you are likely a recovering conformist like me. Regardless of whether I tell myself that I am a rather curious fellow, I find myself slipping at times. Especially when I experience stress. I trust you recognize this.

Curiosity Is Hard

The restaurant story highlights something important. It is hard to be curious all the time. We cannot be curious about the world around us all the time: it would simply take too much energy. It is also hard to be curious about people around us all the time. And is even less likely that we question ourselves regularly. Even though we have no problem in offering others the benefit of our knowledge, we are less ready to let others change our minds, even when the new ideas are better. In the words of behavioural economist and Nobel Prize laureate Daniel Kahneman, "Human beings possess an almost unlimited ability to ignore our ignorance."[4]

One approach to understanding a concept is to juxtapose it against its opposite and see what happens. The challenge is to find the right word. Language is functional, we use language to express our thoughts. Thoughts are more important than words. That's why it is sometimes hard to find the right words for the thoughts we want to express. We often don't think about the extent, depth, and breadth of words like ... curiosity. Even less what its opposite is.

When asking groups what they think the opposite of curiosity is, I often hear words like: "closed-mindedness", "boring", "not interested", "apathy", or "indifference". What would your suggestion be for an antonym of curiosity? Think about it: your answer could provide valuable insights into how you experience curiosity at work and in other aspects of life.

The opposite of curiosity is "conformity".

Now, conformity is a wonderful word. It describes intuitively why it is desirable for me to go back to my favourite Vietnamese restaurant: it feels comfortable; and as long as things don't change, it will remain so.

When things are comfortable, I dial down my curiosity in what restaurant I select. When I have an opinion about something, I resent people who volunteer an alternative view. When I observe a problem at work that is vaguely familiar, I easily jump to a conclusion. Sherlock Holmes had something to say about how easy it is for people to assume they know and disregard what is factual: "It is a capital mistake to theorize before one has data. Insensibly, one begins to twist facts to suit theories, instead of theories to suit facts."

Guises of Conformity

Conformity comes in different guises, We'll go deeper in the different dimensions influencing curiosity in Chapter 4. Let us already discuss the main contours of these dimensions. They are:

- Self-imposed Conformity: The world is a complex place to live in. Work is hard and stressful. In order to cope and decrease the noise around us, we create mental routines and shortcuts to ease ourselves through the day. Often we are even not aware of them. We stick to our preferred brands for our daily needs, listen only to our pre-set channels to access the latest news and eat with the same gang of colleagues at work every day. We don't think of venturing out and changing these routines.

- Team Conformity: Our tribe gives us a sense of belonging and in turn demands loyalty, conformity to rules and beliefs of the team. Failure to do so ends up in potential expulsion.

- Societal Norms: Being part of a society also means adhering to societal norms, i.e., adhering to what society considers good or bad, right or wrong, success or failure.

- Conformity and Technology: Though new technology creates efficiency, it also creates dependence. What would we do without our GPS? Internet technology compounds this effect: algorithms on social media invite us to stay in the cosy echo chambers of like-minded people and prevent us from becoming curious about different-minded people and alternative points of view.

Become aware of all the greater powers that prevent you from showing up curiously and what their consequences are. The more we are aware, the more you will understand the underlying forces, and the more it will empower you. In fact, if you think of a line with conformity on the one end and curiosity on the other, the ideal harmony is not on the side of curiosity, but somewhere in the middle. After all, conformity is not all that bad; we actually need it to get through the day individually, and also to lubricate our social relationships.

Todd Kashdan, Professor of Psychology and Director of the Well-Being Laboratory at George Mason University describes this in a powerful metaphor. "Imagine you're at a fancy dinner party. Everyone's using the salad fork for the salad, so you follow suit. You're not sure why, but it just feels right. This is conformity in action — a social lubricant, reducing friction and making our interactions smoother and more predictable."[5]

Finding a Balance

It is important to recognize when we are conforming out of habit or fear, rather than genuine interest. This requires self-awareness and honesty. It's about asking: "Am I doing this because it's what I truly care about, or because it's what I think is expected of me?" Second, we need to give ourselves permission to be different. This means embracing our quirks, passions, and unique perspectives. It means standing up for what we believe in, even if it goes against the grain.

We also need to communicate our individuality in a way that respects others' expectations. It's about finding ways to express our individuality that enrich our relationships, rather than strain them.

To express ourselves, we need language. Language is a social construct handed on by previous generations. Each word hides historic meaning and cultural connotations. The old phrase 'Curiosity killed the cat' is a good example of an old connotation of curiosity that has been handed down over generations. Until roughly 50 years ago, Curiosity carried negative connotation and was related to looking through keyholes, gossip and questioning the authority of people in power such as elders or managers. Nowadays, curiosity viewed as a positive concept: we want our children to challenge their teachers and actively look for employees who can disrupt the status quo. I encourage you to reflect on what meaning curiosity has in your part of the woods.

Fascinating, right! Hope you are getting warmed up. If you want to go deeper with me and explore the neuroscience of curiosity, join me in the next chapter where we investigate how curiosity is influenced by the inner workings of our mind and brain. Before that, do reflect on the questions below.

Questions for Reflection

- How do you define curiosity in your personal and professional life? How does this definition align with or differ from the three dimensions of curiosity discussed in this chapter?

- Think about a recent situation at work where you faced a complex problem. How did curiosity play a role in finding a solution? If it didn't, how might curiosity have changed your approach?
- Reflect on your current organization or team. How does it encourage or discourage curiosity among its members? What changes could be made to foster a more curious environment?
- Consider a time when you or someone you know demonstrated high levels of intellectual curiosity. What impact did it have on the outcome of the situation?
- In what ways do you currently engage in self-reflective curiosity? How can you enhance your self-awareness to better understand your thoughts, emotions, and motivations?

Notes

1. Eurich, T. (2017). *Insight: The Surprising Truth about How Others See Us, How We See Ourselves, and Why the Answers Matter More Than We Think*. New York: Crown Currency.
2. Folkman, J. (2015). Top ranked leaders know his secret: Ask for feedback. Forbes.com. https://www.forbes.com/sites/joefolkman/2015/01/08/top-ranked-leaders-know-this-secret-ask-for-feedback/ (accessed 29 October 2024).
3. https://www.antwerpen.be/info/cijfers-en-onderzoek-toerisme (accessed 25 September 2024).

4. Kahneman, D. (2011). *Thinking, Fast and Slow*. New York: Macmillan.

5. Kashdan, T. (2023). A new perspective on conformity. Provoked with Dr. Todd Kashdan. https://toddkashdan.sub stack.com/p/a-new-perspective-on-conformity (accessed 25 September 2024).

2

Neuroscience and Curiosity

"Nearly everything is really interesting if you go into it deeply enough."
          Richard Feynman, American theoretical physicist

Trigger Question: which Beatles song stayed longest in the charts?

I will tell you the answer to this question before the end of the chapter, but you might want to avoid the temptation of skipping straight ahead to find the answer. A wealth of scientific research shows that allowing your curiosity to be piqued can be incredibly good for your mind. I encourage you to refrain from doing a Google search and reflect on this question for a short while—and try to find an answer in the vast reserves of experiences and knowledge you have acquired over your lifetime.

Research shows that not knowing the answer to an intriguing question or puzzle can increase your creativity on subsequent tasks, as well as priming your brain for better and deeper learning.[1] Curiosity is so important that it has been found to predict academic achievement, independent of a person's intelligence and grit.

Yet curiosity has received less attention when compared to the terms intelligence and grit. One factor that has hindered a deeper study of curiosity is the lack of a single widely accepted definition of the term. Lynn Burton, host of the successful podcast series *Choose to be Curious*, has interviewed academics, artists, entrepreneurs, and practitioners for over seven years on the topic of curiosity. From more than 200 sessions, she has written down over 250 definitions of the term, such as: "the desire to know", the notion that it has to do with possibility, that it represents an opportunity in the unknown, and that it is inherently optimistic.

Regardless, because of its critical role in the formulation of new perspectives on life and the foundation of science, philosophers and scientists have been intrigued by the concept of curiosity, albeit that not a single book has been dedicated to the subject until now. More recently (in the last 70 years), psychologists have started paying attention to curiosity as they have become interested in the underlying mechanics of child development and learning. It is in this context that William James, the father of modern psychology, defined curiosity as "the impulse towards better cognition", which means it is the desire to understand what is not yet understood.[2]

Another reason is that it has been difficult to study curiosity from the perspective of the single neuron, pathways, and the overall neural brain system. Recent advances, however, have led scholars to link curiosity to neural pathways responsible for executive control, reward, and learning; and have helped us to understand how curiosity relates to information-seeking behaviour, risk taking, and the role of stress and anxiety as a detractor mechanism for curiosity.

Are you still thinking about the question I raised at the start of this chapter? Which Beetles song stayed longest in the charts? Try to notice what happens in your mind. Are you inviting it or are you pushing it away. Does the question create an itch you really want to scratch and find out? Does it bug you that you don't know the answer? Maybe you have already picked up your smartphone and tried to find out the answer. Or have you disregarded the question altogether, considering it not worth a second thought. Or could it be that you know the answer—in which case you also will not be curious?

As we will see, curiosity is mathematically depicted as an inverted U shape: if people have no clue or know the answer, they are not curious. If people know part of the information, they are more likely to respond with curiosity.

Notice also what this question does for your body. What feeling does it spark? I promise you that—if you responded with curiosity to my question—your pupils will have dilated. When we are curious, our body prepares itself to expend energy. One way to observe this is to watch our pupils. The harder the problem, the more dilation.[3]

Novelty and Coping Potential

Researchers have found that when we are triggered by something new, we instinctively answer two questions: (1) is this novel or surprising enough for me to pay attention; and (2) do I have the mental tools to deal with it?

The first question measures the level of surprise the curiosity object represents. If I know the answer, I will not be curious. If this is something that is close to my heart, I will want to know. If not, maybe not.

The first question is what researchers frame as our novelty potential. What you and I consider as novel or surprising might be different and depends on our knowledge, experience, and stress levels.

A little bit of stress makes us look up and pay attention, too much stress paralyzes us and forces us into an incurious fight, flight, or freeze mode.

If you find yourself in a war zone or in a traumatic situation, your survival mode will take over. You will focus on the here and now and block curiosity out. Depression is a good example of a state where people are actively blocking new triggers.

Other mental states, such as hunger, also influence us, even when we don't realize it consciously. In his book *Thinking Fast and Slow*, Daniel Kahneman describes the fact that highly rational court judges in prison parole cases tend to be less lenient to cases just before lunch. The feeling of hunger hijacks our system and makes us less ready to hear why we should be curious about arguments to let inmates go free versus keeping them locked behind bars. Ditto tiredness: when we are tired, we often limit our mental capacities and are less open to new triggers.[4]

The second question refers to assessing the answer to the question of whether I have sufficient mental tools to close my gap in information (aka "coping potential"). These tools are, for instance, our general knowledge or, to a lesser extent, the electronic tools we have at our disposal and support in our environment, like the Google function on our smartphones.

Let's take a deeper look at how curiosity shows up in our brain. Which parts of our brain light up when we show a heightened curiosity? We'll look at three neural pathways: rewards, executive control, and learning.

Curiosity Is Rewarding: The Reward Pathway

Recently, I joined a quiz night out with old friends at our local community centre. An electric atmosphere filled the room. We were anxious as to what the questions were going to be. I observed a competitive battle of minds when I scanned the room. All were trying (or hoping) to outshine others with their superior knowledge. In our group, we beamed with pride every time we knew the answer to a question. Some questions indeed are top of mind and easy. On other questions, especially those in areas where I am not a specialist, I give up. I am not even trying and hope others have the answer. For some questions, I should know the answer, the answer is on the tip of my tongue. For some of them, I can recall the answer quickly, for some I can't. Sometimes uplifting, sometimes frustrating.

Minjeong Kang at Syracuse University in the United States and her peers studied how trivia questions influence curiosity.[5] She gave people MRI scans as they underwent a three-stage experiment. First, she asked people how curious they were about each question. A typical question was: "Which Beatles song stayed longest in the charts?" Choosing between high or low values, people had to indicate how curious they were about the answer. After a short period of time (14 seconds), she shared the correct answer. The last step of the academic exercise was that participants were invited to do a surprise memory test.

Using MRI technology, she measured if and how much the brains of the test subjects lit up when they heard the question the first time, in the time elapsed before knowing the answer, and their reaction when hearing the right answers at the end.

Minjeong Kang found that once curiosity was elicited, two areas in the brains of test subjects started flashing: the midbrain and the nucleus accumbens. Both areas are deep down in the brain. The more a participant wanted to know the answer to the question, the more both these brain regions lit up. Both areas also are linked to the anticipation of reward. In other words, curiosity is a state in which you crave and anticipate a cognitive reward: the information you are curious about.

As it happens, these parts in the brain are part of the dopaminergic pathways, also known as the brain's "wanting system". Researchers found that other areas of this wanting system were also active for the participants. "Wanting system" is an appropriate term: when activated, it makes us want more information and it helps us activate our curiosity and seek this information.

Curiosity turns us into seekers, even when it hurts. Curiosity is often portrayed as a desirable feature of human faculty. In extreme cases, however, the desire to know the answer to a question may come at a cost that sometimes puts people in harmful situations. Researchers have demonstrated that people are indeed willing to take risks, gamble, subject themselves to electric shocks to satisfy their curiosity for trivial knowledge, even when that trivial knowledge has no obvious instrumental value.[6] In such cases, the same brain areas as when we experience hunger are activated: namely the ventral striatum. Sometimes the novelty is so appealing that we are willing to suffer to close our information gap.

Under the right circumstances, humans tend to favour unfamiliar options, as they provide more information. Even though evolutionarily we are conditioned to be risk averse, to conform to the beliefs of the group and to prefer familiarity over unfamiliarity, our brain showcases a preference for novelty.

When given the opportunity, people are more likely to choose novel images over familiar ones, showing a preference for novelty. This preference is expressed as a novelty bonus, which increases expected rewards for novel choices, as indicated by the brain activity in the ventral striatum. This highlights that seeking novelty is intrinsically tied to the brain's reward systems.

Stress is an interesting behaviour when it comes to curiosity. Intuitively, we know that when we are facing a stressful deadline at work, we prefer to block out everything and just get the work done. In those moments, the last thing we want is to think about better ways to do things. Likewise, when we are in a life-threatening situation, stress peaks. In such a case, survival is more important than curiosity. Survival translates into a flight, flight, or freeze response.

On the other hand, when we find ourselves in a low-stress environment, in between two projects at work, when we are visiting the local zoo, or when we are joining a corporate training programme, we feel more ready to learn and be curious. The chemical that regulates our stress is cortisol. With a little stress, small amounts of cortisol are released, causing positive stress, which encourages us to leave our status quo thinking and invites an exploration mindset. Too much stress, on the other hand, initiates a flood of cortisol in our brain and creates a "back away" response. A little bit of stress moves us out of our comfort zone. Too much stress paralyzes.

Executive Control: Attention and Patience

Is the question I raised at the beginning of this chapter still bugging you? If you went online to find the answer, you are probably less curious than you think. Is this maybe counterintuitive? Let me explain.

Recent research from Duke University showed that heightened curiosity meant that people were more willing to wait to find the solution to a puzzle.[7] Less curious people, on the other hand, were more impatient to get through a task quickly, and so they asked to jump straight to the answers. Greater patience and sticking with the problem helped overcome short-term frustration, and led to deeper learning and understanding, particularly when dealing with complex topics. This might also help to explain why curiosity is such a strong predictor of academic success.

"I don't have special talents, I am only passionately curious."

Albert Einstein

If you put your hand above and a little behind your ears, you are covering the parietal lobes of your brain. How would your brain compare to Einstein's brain in this area? In Einstein's brain, the inferior parietal lobe was 15% wider when compared to average people's. The neighbouring region—the parietal operculum—seemed to be missing or smaller in Einstein's brain. It looked like one part of Einstein's brain grew larger, taking over the area that would have been occupied by another part of the brain.

In terms of functionality, the inferior parietal lobe is associated with mathematical thought, visual spatial cognition, and the imagery of movement. Einstein was known to use visual imagination to arrive at his theories. For instance: what would it be like if space-time were curved? What would it be like to ride on a ray of light? The area that was missing is associated with speech production. We know that Einstein did not start talking until he was three. We know that he would obsessively repeat sentences up to the age of seven. We know that he failed the technology institute language exams when he was 16. Einstein always claimed that he thought visually rather than verbally.[8] It is exactly the inferior parietal lobe where the precuneus lies. Researchers have found a correlation between the amount of grey matter in the precuneus and levels of curious and exploratory behaviours.[9]

Attention is important to curiosity because it allows one to selectively focus and concentrate on particular stimuli in the surrounding environment. As there are limited cognitive and sensory resources to understand and evaluate stimuli, attention allows the brain to better focus on what it perceives to be the most important or relevant of these stimuli. Individuals tend to focus on stimuli that are particularly stimulating or engaging. The more attention a stimulus garners, the more frequently one's energy and focus will be directed towards that stimulus. This suggests an individual will focus on new or unfamiliar stimuli in an effort to better understand or make sense of the unknown, rather than on more familiar or repetitive stimuli.

In a study by Kimberley Philips of Trinity College in the US, she and her colleagues found that capuchin monkeys with a greater grey matter density in the precuneus showed more intense responses to unfamiliar objects, a paradigm widely employed as a means to assess curiosity. The precuneus is a region of the brain that is involved in attention, self-awareness, episodic memory, and visuospatial processing.

This finding has an extra twist. Given that the precuneus also monitors self-awareness and meta self-awareness (being aware of our own self-awareness), it actually might help us grow our individual curiosity.[10]

Meditation is also powerful tool to help us. A six-week mindfulness-based intervention was found to correlate with a significant grey matter increase within the precuneus.[11]

Memory and Learning

Given that the standard dictionary definition of curiosity is "the desire to know something", it come as little surprise that much research has been concerned with its benefits for education.

Most of us have memories of our days in school, some good, some bad. Almost always, we have an experience with one teacher who motivated us to learn more. In my case it was Mr Sprengers, my Greek and Latin teacher in secondary school. Learning was so much easier in his presence. When he was around, learning was not a chore, it was fun. His passion rubbed off on us and he made me intrinsically interested in his class. Even more interesting, neuroscience has found that after his class, I would also have been more open to the following teachers' classes. Once we are under a curious spell, we also become more curious about unrelated topics. Why is this?

Remember the trivia experiment? Another objective of Minjeong Kang and her colleagues' experiment was to find out whether curiosity affects learning; more specifically, whether being curious helps in learning information. And if so, why and how. To test this, researchers added a simple step in the experiment. During the 14 seconds waiting time between question and answer, they added a random picture of a neutral person. During the last memory test, participants were tested also on these faces.

What they found was that when people were highly curious to find out the answer to a question, they were not only better at recalling the answer to that question, they also remembered the faces of the random pictures better. When we are curious, we are not only better at learning and remembering the facts that are presented, we also pay more attention to unrelated things. When we are curious, our brains open up to learning any information. Even after time elapses: when checking the memory of the test subjects 24 hours later, they still remembered faces better.[12]

Next time you are conducting a presentation, start with questions; this will ensure your audience pays more attention and remembers your talk better. Or, when you are delivering training, try to build on the already available interest or knowledge of the student to help them open up naturally to the things you want to teach. If teachers want to convey material that is not of general interest, learning is accelerated if the teacher harnesses the power of the student's curiosity about something that they are naturally motivated to learn. This is what great educators understand intuitively. They know how to spark the intellectual curiosity of their students first, which makes them want to receive the information, and, as a result, they retain the information better and longer.

To put you out of your misery: the answer to the Beatles song question is *Hey Jude*.

As we are continuing our journey, I trust you agree with me that "curiosity about curiosity" is becoming more exciting. We have touched upon a number of practical applications already. On top of this, I am sure that you have made your own curious connections and that some lightbulb insights have occurred. Now, how do we become more intentional as professionals? The first step is to allow for it in our lives, our teams, and our organizations. Permission is the first step, which we will cover as soon as you flip to the next chapter.

Questions for Reflection

- Reflect on the connection between curiosity and learning. How can you apply this understanding to improve your own learning processes or those of others?
- Think about a time when you faced a challenging problem. How did curiosity influence your approach to finding a solution?
- How do you balance the need for immediate answers with the benefits of allowing curiosity to guide your learning process?
- In what ways do stress and fatigue impact your curiosity? How can you manage these factors to maintain a curious mindset?
- How does the concept of curiosity as a "wanting system" resonate with your experiences? Can you recall a time when curiosity drove you to take significant risks?

Notes

1. Fell, A. (2014). *Curiosity Helps Learning and Memory*. California: University of California. https://www.univer sityofcalifornia.edu/news/curiosity-helps-learning-and-memory (accessed 30 October 2024).
2. James, W. (1890). *The Principles of Psychology*. Toronto: York University. https://psychclassics.yorku.ca/James/Pri nciples/index.html (accessed 30 October 2024).

3. Hyönä, J., Tommola, J., and Alaja, A.-M. (1995). Pupil dilation as a measure of processing load in simultaneous interpretation and other language tasks. *The Quarterly Journal of Experimental Psychology,* Section A 48 (3): 598–612. https://doi.org/10.1080/14640749508401407 (accessed 30 October 2024).
4. Kahneman, D. (2011). *Thinking, Fast and Slow.* New York: Macmillan.
5. Kang, M.J., Hsu, M., Krajbich, I.M. et al. (2009). The wick in the candle of learning: Epistemic curiosity activates reward circuitry and enhances memory. *Psychological Science* 20 (8): 963–973. https://doi.org/10.1111/j.1467-9280.2009.02402.x (accessed 30 October 2024).
6. Lau, J.K.L., Ozono, H., Kuratomi, K., et al. (2020). Shared striatal activity in decisions to satisfy curiosity and hunger at the risk of electric shocks. *Nature Human Behaviour* 4 (5): 515–523. https://doi.org/10.1038/s41562-020-0848-3 (accessed 30 October 2024).
7. Hsiung, A., Poh, J.-H., Huettel, S.A. et al. (2023). Curiosity evolves as information unfolds. *Proceedings of the National Academy of Sciences* 120 (43): e2301974120. https://doi.org/10.1073/pnas.2301974120 (accessed 30 October 2024).
8. Grim, P. (2008). *Philosophy of Mind: Brians, Consciousness, and Thinking Machines.* The great courses. Audio book. Audible. 2013.
9. Curiosity. https://en.wikipedia.org/wiki/Curiosity (accessed 8 May 2024).
10. Phillips, K.A., Subiaul, F., and Sherwood, C.C. (2012). Curious monkeys have increased gray matter density in the precuneus. *Neuroscience Letters* 518 (2): 172–175. https://doi.org/10.1016/j.neulet.2012.05.004 (accessed 30 October 2024).

11. Kurth, F., Luders, E., Wu, B. et al. (2014). Brain gray matter changes associated with mindfulness meditation in older adults: An exploratory pilot study using voxel-based morphometry. *Neuro* 1 (1): 23–26. doi:10.17140/ NOJ-1-106. PMID: PMC4306280, PMID: 25632405

12. Kang, M.J., Hsu, M., Krajbich, I.M. et al. (2009). The wick in the candle of learning: Epistemic curiosity activates reward circuitry and enhances memory. *Psychological Science* 20 (8): 963–973. https://doi.org/10.1111/j.1467-9280.2009.02402.x (accessed 30 October 2024).

Part 2

The Success Formula of Curiosity

The concepts of permission, awareness, and intentionality are crucial for fostering curiosity at work and at home. Permission involves mustering the courage to take bold steps, reducing anxiety about the unknown, and committing to new ventures. It's essential in both personal relationships and professional environments, as demonstrated by companies like McKinsey and Patagonia that embed curiosity into their values. Awareness focuses on mindfulness and deep engagement with our surroundings, helping us uncover hidden details and insights crucial for strategic decision-making. This involves cultivating self-awareness, situation awareness, and system awareness. Intentionality transforms curiosity into action, driving innovation and satisfaction. Together, these elements enable personal and professional growth, creating a culture of continuous improvement and innovation.

3

Permission

"I believe that the most important single thing,
beyond discipline and creativity ... is daring to
dare."

Maya Angelou, poet and civil rights activist

**Trigger Question: in your opinion, what percentage
of managers say that they invite curiosity in the team?**

I proposed to my wife, Jeltje, in Tibet at the base
camp of Mount Everest.

I had promised myself that the big "Will you
marry me?" question was going to be special. It took
me six months of preparation to plan for the trip and
convince my wife-to-be that visiting Tibet was a better choice than going for a short trip to the Philippines.

When we met, Jeltje and I were both living in
Beijing. We were introduced by my roommate in a
time when there were no mobile phones. She would
call my roommate on a landline for IT support, and
I happened to pick up the phone from time to time.
Jeltje and I found ourselves talking. Time stood still
and we kept talking for long stretches. We still do.
These conversations were the beginning of a relationship that has blessed me for 30 years.

Prepping in my head for the proposal filled me
with excitement, yet I also experienced anxiety. I was
in my mid-20s, at the beginning of life and career.
Not knowing what the future would bring. Was this
the right decision to commit to such a big project—
"till death do us part"? Was I the right person to

make her happy? Was she the one and only? What I knew to be emotionally true, the gremlin in my brain was still trying to examine for loopholes. I remember asking all these gigantic mountains around us to lend me the strength to be a good partner.

Marriage is a good example of when a decision is final. Once the "will you ..." question is popped (and reciprocated), chances are that you commit yourself to staying together, even when times get tough, for better or for worse till death us do part. Luckily for me, Jeltje said "Yes, I do". We hugged for what seemed to be a lifetime, filled with bliss and joy. She was giving me permission. She would only do so because I had given myself permission first.

Permission is all about mustering the courage to take the next courageous step. It is about preparing yourself to jump in the water from a height that is somewhat disturbing and outside your comfort zone. It is about finding the strength to commit to something and say "Yes I do". Permission prepares us for an unknown future. It makes the future less threatening.

Marriage is a good metaphor for giving permission to the future. Permission is the action of officially allowing myself to do a particular thing—I give myself the consent and authorization to be curious, and more importantly, to act on my curiosity.

Research by Daniel Gilbert from Harvard shows that taking a stand helps reduce anxiety more than leaving options open. Professor Gilbert asked people to pick a free poster from a selection of art prints. One group was told they could replace the print if they felt they did not like it after a while. For the other group, the first decision was final. What he found in studying these two groups was that the "final choice" group was more satisfied with decision.[1] When you know you can no longer turn back, anxiety diminishes. Because now there's only one direction to travel, it eliminates the anxiety of rethinking our earlier choices.

Choosing an art print is not entirely the same as a marriage. Marriage requires a string of many permissions over time. If we don't build our relationship, the coziness of a marriage can easily give way to turn into boredom and drifting apart. According to Dr John Gottman, many marriages break down not because of fighting but because the relationship becomes dull and uninteresting.[2]

What typically happens in such relationships is that permission to explore is given at the beginning. After the initial spell of love, conformity sets in. We initially are intensely curious about getting to know the other person; after a while, however, we are convinced we know the other party—at which point exploration subsides. Life takes over and we stop being interested in the love of our life.

Permission is only the first step. We'll discover how to keep our curiosity strong in our relationships. Now, let's focus for a few minutes on the professional side of things.

Permission in the Workplace

Marriage might be familiar territory, but have you ever found yourself in front of a dark cave? Consider the story of Leonardo da Vinci and the dark cave. This story illustrates his curiosity and willingness to confront fear to seek knowledge. He recounts that he found a dark cave and, intrigued by this, squinted and peeked inside hoping he might discover something. When the cave did not surrender any secrets from its depths, he stood at the entrance: "two contrary emotions arose in me, fear and desire — fear of the threatening dark cavern, desire to see whether there were any marvelous things within it."[3]

Have you ever felt you were standing in the same position as Leonardo? A situation which created both anxiety as well as a yearning? If you are like me, you will have many such instances, even daily. Even about simple things: do I buy this new vegetable? I have heard it is healthy and delicious, yet I don't know how to prepare it. Do I suggest this new idea to the team? I think it would greatly improve things around here, yet maybe they tried this before and my manager did not appreciate my earlier suggestion? Do I volunteer for this new challenging project, knowing I need to give up the cosy environment and great team I am part of now? As a leader, do I invite dissenting views in the team, knowing it can improve engagement and productivity, yet invite inefficiencies?

At such moments, we have the choice to either lean in to our anxiety and allow ourselves to explore the unknown, or else revert to the easy and comfortable safe space of the known status quo. Not doing anything is easy. Saying "no" to our impulses is the path of least resistance. Our brains are hardwired to worry and remain in the comfortable space of the known world. This happens even at the unconscious level.

Are we giving in to our anxiety and playing it safe, or are we leaning in to our anxiety and exploring? In the words of the Buddhist nun Pema Chodron:

"Let your curiosity be greater than your fear."

You will find that it is easier to do so when you are in a calm mental place. If you are stressed or not in balance, you will find yourself less ready to give permission to curiosity. A good example is stress created by hunger: hunger negatively affects rational decision-making in food shopping, leading to impulsive buying behaviour and increased purchasing of high-sugar and high-fat foods. In 2013, researchers Tal and Wansink wrote an academic paper with a telling title: "Fattening Fasting: Hungry Grocery Shoppers Buy More Calories, Not More Food". In essence, if you walk around hungry in a supermarket, you will be much more prone to buy things you don't need.[4]

You can also think of work-related stress, such as a project deadline or a toxic atmosphere that doesn't contribute to a willingness to go the extra mile. Remember that curiosity requires energy to move us away from the gravitational pull of conformity. Curiosity is about seeking; conformity is about keeping. It is easier to keep than to seek.

When I teach curiosity to leaders, I sometimes ask people to participate in a thought experiment I learned from Cecile Cremer, futurist and trend expert, when she and I were speaking at the same event in 2021. I present a picture of an alien (an egg-like head with two eyes, two dots for a nose, and a simple mouth) and invite people to draw their own version of an alien. The caveat is that I add stress to the equation, and only give the audience 60 seconds. Once the time is up, I ask people how many have drawn something similar to the picture I showed. Many hands go up. When we are stressed, we become less imaginative and go with what is right in front of us, especially when it looks familiar and acceptable. When in stress, we are less likely to think out of the box.

Cecile Cremer explained to me that in her line of work—trend watching —it is hard to break away from the known familiar world and think of a future without being limited by the lenses of today. It is hard to imagine a future which is not a version of today. This is hard for even the brightest minds. The French author Jules Verne wrote wonderful futuristic stories, yet he never imagined that humanity would invent mobile telephones and that we would use these devices to look at cats or new food recipes. Being an extraordinary thinker, he came close though. In his novel *Paris in the Twentieth Century*, written in 1863 but not published until 1994, Verne described the dystopian world of Paris in the 1960s. A world with advanced technology that includes a communication device capable of sending written messages over long distances.[5] Most of us are not as forward looking as Jules Verne, especially when we are stressed.

Or when we think we know something.

The more we consider ourselves to be experts, the less we open ourselves up to alternative future scenarios. I have seen many executives who prided themselves on having lots of experience, and because of this did not allow team members to swim outside of their lanes or come up with ideas for positive change. Kodak could not imagine that digital photography would be a thing, RIM could not imagine that the BlackBerry could be used for more than just secure corporate emails and business communication. I am sure you have your own examples of where hubris has prevented others, or even yourself, from exploring new paths.

At the most basic level, curiosity is making the gap between the known and the unknown easier to cross. Curiosity helps us to step out of our comfort zone. It is the tool to explore our own strengths and flaws. It strengthens our relationships, gives meaning to the evolving world around us; it makes technology less threatening and it opens up some of the mysteries around us. The thing is, for most of us, this is hard and permission is the first step.

Being curious is like saying "Yes, I do". When compared to remaining idle, it is harder, takes more energy, and we momentarily feel some loss of power. Yet if we do indeed lean into our anxiety, magic happens. Permission, as in my marriage proposal, can make us wobble on our legs, can make us humble and vulnerable; can cause us stress, yet I promise you, it is liberating. It builds confidence. It is almost like a spiritual experience where you give yourself over to a higher power.

The Power of Systemic Permission

Beyond individuals, systems can give permission too. Take communities: the first 3 of the 12 steps of the Alcoholics Anonymous organization require their members to give permission as the foundation for giving up alcohol, namely Step 1: Admit your life has become unmanageable. Step 2: Accept that you need God to become sober and Step 3: Decide to turn over your life to God. Their 12 spiritual principles of recovery are as follows: acceptance, hope, faith, courage, honesty, patience, humility, willingness, brotherly love, integrity, self-discipline, and service.[6] Permission is indeed the first step for them: permission to take a new life direction, permission to let go of past behaviours, and permission to be assisted along the way. If you are a non-religious person, you might frown at the reference to God; however, research has shown that delegating one's troubles to a higher power can be liberating.

Permission at the Country Level

Permission for curiosity can also be found at the country level: compare North Korea with South Korea and intuitively we can grasp which of these two countries is giving more permission to its citizens to explore themselves, relationships, and the world at large. Countries or communities where politics or religion enter deep into the homes of their citizens tend to favour conformity more than curiosity.

Permission at the Company Level

Companies are also in the business of giving permission. Permission in companies is structured around corporate values and what type of behaviour is encouraged and what is not. In terms of curiosity, the more company leadership creates a conducive environment for it, the more people will feel empowered. I became aware of the power of corporate permission during a culture change programme at the IT services giant Cognizant, where I was Chief Learning Officer. We had launched a new learning culture, one where we changed the paradigm of employee learning from one of compliance and to one driven by a combination of what the company needed and the employee's own drive. We communicated our new strategy to all 300,000 employees and invited them to deepen the skills required in their roles, and also to prepare themselves for their next role.

The CEO at the time, Brian Humpfries, and the executive team supported the initiative, even deciding to double the company's learning and development budget to close to 100 million dollars. I communicated this message around the company, as did Humpfries, to encourage employees to find the openness, wonder, and drive to start learning new things. This permission was crucial to setting the scene for the organization and kickstarting the programme. (We will discuss later that permission was only the first key step.)

In my view, the highest level of permission is given at the level of corporate values. By including curiosity in the flow of desired values and behaviours in the organization, companies display to employees, shareholders, and stakeholders that permission is automatically granted for the concepts they list.

Companies like Netflix, Novartis, Dell, Nasa, and Disney have adopted "curiosity" as a specific identifier in their corporate values. They openly state that they value curiosity in the workplace. Other companies equally value curiosity yet use other terminology to describe their cultural preference for exploration and inquisitiveness; for example:

- Patagonia: "Not bound by convention—Our success—and much of the fun—lies in developing new ways to do things."[7]
- TikTok: "Always day one." This reminds them to keep an entrepreneurial mindset whilst also being humble and not complacent about past achievements.[8]
- Unilever: "Pioneering." Unilever encourages innovation, creativity, and a forward-thinking mindset. The company continually seeks new ways to improve its products, processes, and operations, embracing change and driving progress.[9]
- Zappos: "Be Adventurous, Creative, and Open-Minded." This encourages employees to explore new ideas and take risks in a supportive environment.[10]

McKinsey and company is another example that I described in my first book *The Workplace Curiosity Manifesto*. They tout "the obligation to dissent" as a value. Employees at McKinsey are not only invited to challenge the status quo, be curious and articulate it; they are obliged to do so, even when this means challenging the status quo in front of seniors. When asking Rob Theunissen, partner in the company's European organizational practice, whether this value is more than just lip service, he shared with me that this value is taken very seriously and underscored: "At McKinsey tension is a good thing. Honesty trumps harmony, every day."

Companies like Patagonia and McKinsey are the minority. The fact of the matter is that deep down organizations are more at ease with status quo thinking than with challenging it. According to Professor Andre Wierdsma, companies are modelled on the example of army and church. Throughout the ages, army and church have been known to operate more in a paradigm of conformist thinking than curiosity. Both systems are rigidly structured around hierarchy, separation of knowledge across levels, the expectation of loyalty and discipline in return for job security, separation of thinking and doing, and an overall drive to maintain the status quo. Companies are designed on their template.[11]

The place where culture and values are lived and experienced the most is the team. In teams, the role of the leader as role model is key to encouraging a conducive curiosity culture. When I ask leaders whether curiosity is a good thing, 90% answer in the affirmative with a yes. When I then correlate this answer to another question, namely "whether they are giving permission to their own team to challenge the status quo and explore", only 50% reply that they do. This highlights the difference between theory and practice. In theory, leaders welcome the idea. In practice, however, we prefer the other departments to stick out their necks, fearing that allowing for curiosity will destabilize the group and lead to loss of efficiency.

This is the answer to the question at the head of this chapter. What was your answer? We'll dive deeper into this conundrum in Chapter 10, "Leadership and Curiosity".

I'll make the case later in this book that in times of change we cannot afford not to give permission to challenge the status quo. So, what's the opportunity cost if leaders do not give permission to their teams to be curious, ask questions, and challenge? Here are some ideas:

- Innovation Loss: Suppressed curiosity limits the potential for innovation and unique ideas.
- Employee Engagement: Without encouragement to question, employee engagement and productivity may decrease.
- Continuous Improvement: Discouraging challenging behaviour stifles opportunities for process or product improvement.
- Strategic Decision-making: Limited questioning can narrow perspectives and impair strategic decision-making.
- Risk Management: Without challenges, potential risks or flaws may go unnoticed and unaddressed.

- Learning and Growth: A lack of curiosity can lead to stagnation in skills and knowledge expansion.
- Talent Retention: A non-stimulating environment may push top talents towards more intellectually encouraging competitors.
- Customer Satisfaction: Without question-based problem solving, customer satisfaction may suffer.

Now that you have given yourself permission, you are ready to prepare your muscles for the jump. You can better jump farther when you first take a few steps back. In French, there is an appropriate saying for this. "*Il faut reculer pour mieux sauter*". You have to take a step back sometimes to allow yourself to better analyze the situation and therefore prepare the groundwork for new things. We'll cover this in the next chapter.

Are you ready to become more aware?

Questions for Reflection

- How do you currently give yourself permission to explore new ideas and take risks in your professional life?
- Can you identify a recent situation where making a final decision reduced your anxiety? How did this impact your effectiveness?
- In what ways do you encourage continuous curiosity within your team or organization?

- Reflect on a time when you hesitated to express a new idea at work. What were the reasons, and how could you have approached it differently?
- How do you ensure that curiosity remains a core value in your organization's culture?

Notes

1. Burkeman, O. (2021). *Four Thousand Weeks: Time Management for Mortals*. New York: Farrar, Straus and Giroux.
2. Gottman, J.M. and Silver, N. (1999). *The Seven Principles for Making Marriage Work*. New York: Three Rivers Press.
3. Da Vinci, L. (1956). *The Notebooks of Leonardo Da Vinci* (Vol. I & II, J. P. Richter, Ed.). New York: Dover Publications.
4. Tal, A. and Wansink, B. (2013). Fattening fasting: Hungry grocery shoppers buy more calories, not more food. *JAMA Internal Medicine* 173 (12): 1146–1148. doi:10.1001/jamainternmed.2013.650
5. Verne, J. (1994). *Paris in the Twentieth Century* (R. Howard, Trans.). New York: Random House. (Original work written in 1863.)
6. https://goodlandingrecovery.com/what-are-the-12-steps-to-recovery/ (accessed 25 September 2024).
7. https://www.patagonia.com/mx/core-values/ (accessed 25 September 2024).
8. https://www.brightnetwork.co.uk/employer-advice/tiktok/tiktoks-values/ (accessed 25 September 2024).
9. Boardmix. (2024). *Unilever Mission and Vision Statement Analysis*. https://boardmix.com/analysis/unilever-mission-and-vision-statement-analysis/#:~:text=A%20pioneerin

g%20spirit%20has%20been,it%20to%20navigate%20 uncharted%20territories (accessed 24 September 2024).

10. Zappos! About Us. https://www.zappos.com/c/about (accessed 24 September 2024).

11. Wierdsma, A. and Swieringa, J. (2011). *Lerend organiseren en veranderen.* Groningen: Noordhoff Uitgevers.

4

Awareness

"This space that has been granted to us rushes by so speedily and so swiftly that all save a very few find life at an end just when they are getting ready to live."

Lucius Annaeus Seneca, Roman Stoic
philosopher and statesman

Trigger Question: how self-aware are you when you are stressed?

When was the last time you went to a museum and looked at a piece of art in a gallery, or a statue in the city? Chances are that you spent little time paying deep attention. Research at likely one of most impressive art temples in the world, the National Gallery in London, found that visitors spend a mere four seconds looking at the art they came to see. What is preventing people from spending more time looking at the masterpieces of world-famous artists like Van Eyck, Turner, Leonardo da Vinci, Seurat, and others? Is it the two dimensionality of a painting? Is it that visitors are overwhelmed by the number of art works and need to divide the limited time they have?

Or is it that we don't take time to slow down?

In this chapter, we will focus on why it is so important to slow down, breathe, and pay attention. When we do, hidden details and beauty reveal themselves to us. Things that we would miss otherwise.

Big and small; like, for instance, paying attention to weak market signals in designing new products, noticing collective biases in the team which prevents it from high performance. Or not noticing the plank in our own eye while trying to take out the speck of sawdust in your brother's eye. Becoming aware is the key to liberation.

While we are in the good company of the masters of the National Gallery museum, what happens if we dial up the appeal of an artwork with extra sensory stimuli, like adding sound and turning it into a story?

Chris Watson is President of the Wildlife Recording Society, a group of passionate sound nerds and engineers. He is not just any wildlife recording buff, he also happens to be the sound engineer for Sir Richard Attenborough, the god of nature documentaries. Mr Watson was contacted by the National Gallery in London with the request to think out of the box and see what he could do help extend the four seconds people spend appreciating their masterpieces. Intrigued by this request, he promised to help, even though Mr Watson in his own words is anything but an art specialist. He hypothesized that adding sound might help and put this thought to the test with "The Corn Field", a painting by the British nineteenth-century painter John Constable. He created a three-minute recording of the sound of elements appearing in the painting—church bells, horses, dogs, the wind, and the babble of a stream—to turn the painting into a multimedia experience. Creating sound resulted in people spending four minutes instead of four seconds. A huge improvement.[1]

Paying Attention

Most people don't start their days with mindful awareness. If you are like me, I often cannot remember later in the day all the thoughts that enter my mind in the morning, or what I had for breakfast. Or what my partner has decided to wear for the day. It's normal—unless we pay extra attention, we are oblivious to so many things. Me too, I am guilty as charged.

What is your story of today, or of any workday? How much are you going through your day on automatic pilot?

In the practice of mindfulness, *single focus* is a big thing. Single focus helps us to pay attention to the very thing we are doing. If you are walking, focus on walking and nothing else. So, no listening to an audiobook, checking your social media stream, talking to another person, or even daydreaming. Just walking. When you walk mindfully, you walk and concentrate on walking. You observe yourself walking, feel your muscles, the ground under your feet, the colours around you, your breathing. Have you ever asked yourself how many steps you can take on one exhale, and how many you take on one inhale?

Most people wake up to a daily routine: shower, dress, etc. My wife has started taking cold showers every day. She tells me this is a great thing to wake her up—really wake her up. Not only her body, but also her mind. Looking for extremes helps us become aware of the comfortable middle ground.

Unless you are using a GPS to go to work, most of us take the same route to our office (or favourite shop). When that route is not available, we can become annoyed; not at the road, but at ourselves because at that point we are forced to consider new options. Being on autopilot was so much more comfortable and easier. Thinking about new possibilities takes more energy. Curiosity takes more energy.

After all, we need structure in our lives. If something is good, why change? Conforming to what we know and believe to be true makes life easier to handle in the hustle and bustle of everyday life. It gives us one less extra thing to worry about. It gives us a sense of predictability and control. This is fine when we find ourselves on stable ground. As soon as there is change around us, the truth of yesterday might not be useful for today anymore.

The more we become aware of the conformist narratives we tell ourselves, or the stories we are led to believe and follow through the environment we're in, the stronger we are in facing and accepting change. Becoming aware is hard as the insights we gain might tell us a different story than the one we are used to or feel comfortable with. It might also unearth some unconscious beliefs we have about the world, others or even ourselves.

Becoming aware is a superpower. Without it, it is hard to acquire the right data points to change course. I find it useful to deconstruct language in order to get to the core of what we understand by something. I agree with Amy Edmondson (professor at Harvard Business School and author many books, her latest being *The Right Kind of Wrong, The Science of Failing Well*) that there are three different types of awareness[2]:

- There is *self-awareness*, our human capacity for sustained self-reflection, humility, honesty, and curiosity, which propels us to seek out patterns that provide insight into our behaviour.

- There is also *situation awareness*, that is our ability to read a given external situation and judge its potential outcome. When I see my neighbour cutting the big tree on the border of our property, I am able to predict a couple of outcomes, including judging whether the tree will fall on my house or not.

- The third type of awareness is *system awareness*. System awareness refers to an—often intuitive—understanding of complex systems where our actions trigger unintended consequences. Learning to read and appreciate systems—organizations, nature, family systems—helps us understand them.

Slowing Down

How does this all connect to the earlier discussion of looking at a painting? What happens if you were asked to spend three hours viewing the same painting, without the added feature of rural sounds and without the distractive power of a smart phone? Quite a daunting task, right? Torturous even. This is an assignment Jennifer Roberts, who teaches art history at Harvard University, gives each of her students every year. Each student chooses a painting or piece of art in a local museum, then goes and looks at it for three hours straight. Three hours. Let that sink in for a moment: no checking email or social media; no quick runs to a coffee shop. The objective of the exercise is for people to become one with the painting. Once they are, they see the painting through different eyes.[3]

It will come as no surprise that students hate this exercise and react with disbelief when they hear first of it. Claire Bown, the founder of the Thinking Museum and a slow-looking teacher for museum guides around the world, confirmed this when I spoke to her: "Not rushing things can be excruciating at first, especially for modern people accustomed to speed. Yet eventually people get used to it. Once people have gotten beyond their initial frustration, they slow down and start noticing different aspects of the artwork, subtle expressions, and they get drawn into the picture. Slow-looking helps us 'step back' to more clearly see the world around us, our relationships and ourselves. There is power in stepping back. The only way to approach it is with humility."

Being superficially aware is easy. Being deeply aware is a whole different kettle of fish. Tasha Eurich, self-awareness researcher, is correct when she says that 90% of people say they are self-aware, yet only

10% really are. After all, we delude ourselves into the belief that we know who we are, why we are right, and why others aren't. Becoming aware makes us tap in to who we really are and invites us to take decisions at a deeper level.

I encourage you to "slow down and observe". In my earlier book, *The Workplace Curiosity Manifesto*, I described this dimension as "question your teaspoons". What I meant by this was to develop a new kind of attention, to the banal, the quotidian, to the world, life, others, ourselves in order to live our daily experiences differently. Regularly taking time off is important also in the corporate world. Taking time to connect, to discuss, to collectively slow down, to take regular collective time off; not with the intention to discuss operational issues, but the deeper whys and hows of life in general.

Curiosity requires courage. The courage to get real with yourself, to acknowledge your internal stories. Taking this idea one step further, in a society that encourages us to be focused on being rational, we are more aware of our thinking processes than what happens at the physical level. Many people have forgotten how to feel, how to listen to their bodies, or to their intuition. In our rational society, we are more aware of our thinking processes than what happens at the physical level.

What about slowing down now? Sit down, observe your breath and listen to your body. What does your body tell you?

Four Reasons Why Awareness Is Hard

The reason why stepping back, observing, and becoming aware is hard is best understood though the understanding of curiosity's polar opposite: conformity, discussed earlier. While conformity is about keeping, curiosity is about seeking. Curiosity is about playing-to-win; conformity is about playing-not-to-loose. Curiosity is about expanding our horizon; conformity is about being right.

In the right dose, a state of conformity is good. Taking the same road to work every day feels good. We don't have to strain our brains to think of an alternative route and can prepare ourselves for the day ahead. Conformity is good in social interactions as it creates the minimal rules of engagement to have a good time together. Product conformity is appreciated by customers who want the same product today that they bought earlier.

High levels of conformity can be toxic and counterintuitive. At a recent conference, a participant came to me after my keynote. He shared that my talk had made a profound impact on him, and it had got him reflecting on the climate in his professional setting: a global chemical company. He continued: "In our company, we need 700 signatures to change a process. As a result, we are collectively paralyzed to look for improvements, even small ones." This example highlights that excessive levels of conformity are also the worst means to deal with change. Once we are in a high conformity zone, we don't see new opportunities or alternative paths and block out innovation. In such a state, we stop asking questions and are not interested in looking under the hood.

There are four reasons why conformity often has the upper hand over curiosity. We discussed the different guises of conformity earlier in Chapter 1. Let us discuss this in more depth.

First, there is the conformity that we impose on ourselves. This can have mental or physical underlying processes. We are often not aware of our self-imposed conformity drivers. In the hustle and bustle of everyday life and work, we create automatic routines to get us through the day. We find ourselves taking the same road to our office, we go to the same store to buy stuff, take the same track when we walk the dog and hang out with the same gang of familiar people, and prefer to go to the same restaurant. Also, we push away new ideas people might suggest, especially if these thoughts are not in sync with our view of the world. Conformity to our beliefs and routines gives us a feeling of being in control, of predictability in an otherwise hostile, stressful and unpredictable world. This strategy is necessary for us, as it keeps us sane. Challenging our status quo takes energy. To be curious takes energy.

The second reason why conformity is strong happens at the level of the team. Since the dawn of time, the strength of the homo sapiens species has been one of numbers. The tribe we belonged to has given us protection, identity, friendship and meaning. The more we lived and worked in groups, the better chances we had of survival. In such a system, loyalty and obedience to group norms are the surest way not to be kicked out of the tribe and risk an uncertain death. In every modern team we can find this group dynamic, even in senior executive teams. The economist John Galbraith rightly said: "In any great organization it is far, far safer to be wrong with the majority than to be right alone."[4]

The third pull of conformity happens at the level of the larger group or the (sub)society. Written rules are needed to keep order in society. We would not want people to decide for themselves which side of the road they'd prefer to drive on. In every larger group, there are also a myriad of unwritten rules about what is considered good and bad, what is considered right or wrong, desirable or undesirable. Sometimes silly rules are dead serious, such as whether the man can be smaller in size than his partner, whether same-sex partners can hold hands on the street, how people should interact with authority figures, or the type of car that screams success.

The last and final conformity trigger is technical in nature: algorithms on social media which persuade us to stay in the same echo-chamber. Social media algorithms wield persuasive influence, shaping the information accessible to users and even impacting voting decisions. This is referred to as persuasive technology, a design approach that aims to modify behaviour by exploiting emotional and psychological responses. Notably, Facebook's algorithm has been shown to prefer content in newsfeeds that triggers heightened emotional reactions, a strategy intended to prolong user engagement on the platform.[5] Moreover, various machine-learning algorithms employed by social media companies prioritize high-engagement content rather than less exciting true information, often neglecting considerations for misinformation.[6] This imbalance contributes to the following alarming trend: A study by MIT found that false news spreads significantly faster on X (previously Twitter) compared to legitimate news. Specifically, false information spreads six times faster than true information on the platform, highlighting the efficiency with which misinformation can proliferate.[7]

Forms of Conformity: Judgement and Bullshit

Becoming aware opens a new reality, one which we have often hitherto been unaware of.

Judgement is an unconscious reaction to a conscious situation. We observe a physical or mental action and compare it to our own frame of reference. When we consider that a bicycle is a better means of transport than an SUV in a city, we might frown upon the driver of an SUV trying to park their car in a narrow spot. Or when someone in the team suggests something new which disagrees with how I think things should be handled, I might block the suggestion. When the thing in front of us fits our way of perceiving things, we nod in agreement. When it doesn't, we judge the other person for being different, or not loyal, or disruptive.

Judgement, and the lack of it, can lead to business decline—as highlighted in the following Budweiser case. In 2023, Bud Light faced significant backlash after partnering with transgender influencer Dylan Mulvaney as part of their marketing campaign. The campaign, which included sending Mulvaney a personalized can of Bud Light to celebrate her one-year anniversary of transitioning, aimed to promote diversity and inclusivity. However, it sparked a strong negative reaction from some consumers and conservative commentators, who accused the brand of alienating its traditional customer base. This controversy led to calls for boycotts, resulting in a notable decline in sales and a substantial impact on the brand's public image and market performance. Bud Light lost its status as the top-selling beer in the United States—a spot it had held for 20 years.[8] A good example of an incurious assumption of Bud's marketing team and a judgemental reaction from its customer base.

Bullshit, on the other hand, is a conscious conformist reaction to a conscious situation. In the words of the philosopher Harry Frankfurt: "Bullshit is worse than lying. It is making statements not to deliberately deceive, but simply with an effort to impress, and with utter disregard for the truth."[9] So while, to some extent, arrogance is inevitable, the big danger is when it becomes so pervasive that people no longer realize they are even displaying it. When we believe the words we say, we stop being curious.

Curious workplaces are defined by leaders who care to know the truth about the impact they are having and who continuously seek feedback from people who will give them the truth. Not easy when power is added to the mix.

Instead of questioning underlying beliefs, examining blind spots, celebrating situations where "I don't know" doesn't equal ignorance but self-awareness and confident humility, the truth is that overconfidence, and even dishonesty, are often reliable attributes for winning and retaining power. This is especially true in environments dominated by political agendas. Or stress.

The Influence of Stress on Curiosity

When do you find yourself in the mood to read a book, to take a stroll in the park, to explore a new cuisine? In short: when are the circumstances right for you to be curious? I often ask a version of this question when working with teams. By a show of hands, who reads more books on holidays than outside of holidays? What is your answer? An overwhelming majority read books, spend more quality time with their partner, and are interested in exploring new stuff when on holiday.

Even when we tell ourselves we are more curious than our neighbour, when our daily plate of required activities is full, we have less head space to be curious. Stress compounds this. A little bit of stress gets us outside our comfort zone and primes us to activate our curiosity. A lot of stress has the opposite effect. It paralyzes us. When we experience too much stress, any stress—relational stress, deadlines at work—we risk showing less curiosity. Though there are differences in how much stress people can handle, at some point we all have a breaking point beyond which we stop being curious. This ability to deal with stress can be measured. It is called stress tolerance. If you take the curiosity diagnostic which is introduced at the end of the next chapter, you'll get a score on your level of stress tolerance. A high score means that you can maintain your curiosity to a relatively high level of stress. A low stress tolerance score means the opposite; in this case, stress paralyzes even in a small dose.

Reflect on the trigger question of this chapter: how self-aware are you when you are stressed? Become aware of your stress triggers. Ask yourself: which situations give me the right type of stress that helps me perform better versus the type of stress that paralyzes me? Stress (or anger) may be a response to a value of yours that's being threatened. Maybe you really value collaboration, but your team is struggling to innovate together. Anxiety is a common response when we don't have all the answers or can't see the path ahead. If your organization is going through a transition, you may be feeling anxious.

That's normal. Ask yourself what's in your control and what isn't and figure out how you can live by your values even in the midst of change.

Why Curiosity Declines Over Time

When we are too long in a job, we risk losing some of our initial curiosity. My research tells me that people who spend longer than three years in the same job risk becoming less curious. I consulted a large multi-national company recently where the board had just approved an aggressive growth plan. I invited the top 200 executives of the firm to take part in a curiosity assessment. I do this often; it gives me a way to understand the company better. The executives love it because I give each of them an in-depth report of their curiosity quotient spanning 10 dimensions. They love the data as much as I do. What I noticed with this group was that quite a number of the most senior team had spent 8–12 years in the same role. When I looked at "years in role" and plotted the 10 dimensions, I noticed a declining trend in the category of one of the dimensions in the report: calculated risk taking.

While curiosity is about playing to win, conformity is about playing not to lose. In the beginning, we are curious; only to see its power diminished over time when we stop exploring and think we have all the answers. Or when we become afraid to ask, thinking that we should know.

The CEO took these findings to heart and she started taking mitigation steps, such as introducing a job rotation policy after three years of tenure for all levels. The job rotation policy states that after three years, people are required to move around unless there is a sound reason not to do so (and the reasoning is reviewed yearly to be sure it still applies). As a result, succession planning immediately was also taken much more seriously.

Become aware is not a "nice to have" if you want to become a better version of yourself, it's a "have to have". It helps you tune in to your underlying belief systems and routines. Pay attention to why we say the things we say, do the things we do, and think the things we think. Become aware of what excites us and what doesn't. What gives us energy and what drains it. What stories do I tell myself about why things can (or cannot) be done. At a team level, explore the language we use and the questions we ask; for instance, are we asking questions to which we know the answers already or are we inviting new questions?

Permission gets us going and lays the foundation for us to go deep, slow down, and become aware. Equipped with the insights we have gained along the way, we find ourselves in front of two options. The first option might be that we decide that the current status quo is good as it is. The other option decides that the time is ripe and the stars aligned to take action. That is what we are going to discuss in the next chapter.

Questions for Reflection

- How often do you find yourself rushing through tasks without fully engaging in them? What impact does this have on your work and overall productivity?
- Can you identify any weak market signals or subtle changes in your industry that you might be overlooking?
- What are your stress triggers at work, and how do they impact your ability to stay curious and aware? What strategies can you implement to manage this stress effectively?
- How can you encourage a culture of mindfulness and awareness within your team or organization? What specific practices or initiatives could support this goal?
- Reflect on a recent situation where conformity within your organization stifled innovation. How could increased awareness have changed the outcome?

Notes

1. Watson, C. (2015). The sound of story. https://www. youtube.com/watch?v=EC2CKEHu_lQ (accessed 25 September 2024).
2. Edmondson, A.C. (2023). *The Right Kind of Wrong: The Science of Failing Well*. Atria books. New York: Simon and Schuster.

3. Roberts, J. (2013). The power of patience: Teaching students the value of deceleration and immersive attention. *Harvard Magazine* 116 (2): 40–43.

4. Burgers, W. (2008). *Marketing Revealed: Challenging the Myths*. New York: Palgrave MacMillan.

5. Chakradhar, S. (2021). More internal documents show how Facebook's algorithm prioritized anger and posts that triggered it. *NiemanLab*. https://www.niemanlab.org/2021/10/more-internal-documents-show-how-facebooks-algorithm-prioritized-anger-and-posts-that-triggered-it/ (accessed 30 October 2024).

6. Milli, S., Carroll, M., Wang, Y. et al. (January 3, 2024). Engagement, user satisfaction, and the amplification of divisive content on social media. *Knight First Amendment Institute*. Retrieved from https://knightcolumbia.org/content/engagement-user-satisfaction-and-the-amplification-of-divisive-content-on-social-media (accessed 30 October 2024).

7. Vosoughi, S., Roy, D. and Aral, S. (2018). The spread of true and false news online. *Science* 359 (6380): 1146–1151. https://www.science.org/doi/10.1126/science.aap9559 (accessed 30 October 2024).

8. Holpuch, A. (2023). Behind the backlash behind Bud Light. *New York Times*. https://www.nytimes.com/article/bud-light-boycott.html (accessed 30 October 2024).

9. Frankfurt, H.G. (2005). *On Bullshit*. Princeton: Princeton University Press.

5

Intentionality

"Tell me, what is it you plan to do with your one
wild and precious life?"

Mary Oliver, Poet

**Trigger Question: if you put a frog in cold water and
gradually heat up the water, will the frog let itself
boil to death?**

Curiosity is all about bringing ideas to life.
Having an idea and then acting on it, believing
in it, staying the course, being open to learning,
thinking that you can always improve. Here's an
example from the world of ice-skating.

The Iceland Skating Rink in Hynes, California
opened on 3 January 1940, at the height of World
War II. It was an instant hit. People were looking for
a happy distraction, and ice skating was popular at
the time. Yet, the skating business was tricky.
Resurfacing the ice was labour intensive, involving
manual tools like planers, hoses, and squeegees.
Resurfacing took five people around an hour and a
half to complete.

Frank Zamboni did not like to skate, yet he saw
an opportunity. He invented and designed a self-
propelled resurfacing machine. In 1942, he bought a
farm tractor and experimented with modifications,
testing them at the rink whenever he had the chance.
In 1949, after multiple prototypes, Frank took to the
ice with his Zamboni Model A and resurfaced his
20,000-square-foot rink in 10 minutes. The lesson

here is to never settle for the status quo, even if you don't like skating; like Frank Zamboni, who named this new machine after himself.

In 1954, the Boston Bruins became the first NHL team to purchase a Zamboni, and by 1957, the NCAA had determined that all new rinks would accommodate the machine.[1] In 1960, Zambonis made their first appearance at the Winter Olympics.[2] To date, more than 13,000 Zamboni machines have been sold around the world.[3]

The lesson is that he was intentional. He reimagined how a tractor could be repurposed to solve a different problem. Inventing things gave him energy. This chapter will expand on how such energy can be harnessed through intentional action. Curiosity, at least the type of curiosity we are discussing here, requires proactive action. Consider the word "curiosity" to be a verb, which presupposes taking initiative. Curiosity is not curiosity unless we act upon it. Permission allows us to explore new territories, awareness gives us the tools, and intentionality makes us act.

What Gives Us Energy?

As a kid at school, I loved to let a balloon fly off with a message hoping that someone would send it back. Nobody ever did send back a message that they had received it, yet this did not ruin the excitement of seeing the balloon fly off. The master storyteller Stephen Shepard shared with me a similar story: he had encountered a 104-year-old man in Dallas, whose hobby was to bind messages to tumbleweed bushes and let them go, hoping people would contact him. People did; not often, but they did. Once he was even contacted by someone 160 kilometres away. The old man found meaning and fun in this novel hobby.

In 2007, Nobel laureate Daniel Khaneman and Princeton economist Alan Krueger published a paper called: "Are We Having More Fun Yet". They wanted to find out whether massive social progress, technological advancement, and the economic prosperity of the last 50 years had actually increased our satisfaction and meaning in life. One would hope that with numerous new helpers like dishwashers around the house, as well as efficiency enhancing tools such as GPS and smartphones, we would be able to spend more time doing what we care about most.

Strangely enough, it doesn't. The answer to Khaneman's and Krueger's question is a resounding "No!" Most people spend less than 20% of their days doing what they could term "meaningful activity", such as being with close friends, playing, lovemaking, spiritual practice, or even sending out tumbleweeds into the world.[4]

It does not have to be this way. Curiosity can come to the rescue if we let it enter our lives. Curiosity has the potential to trigger us to experience the world differently. It even has the power to enhance our appreciation of the world and people around us, even appreciation of ourselves. We only need to give it permission, become aware of its presence, and then take an intentional stand.

Intentionality can also be experienced in teams and organizations. Let's take sustainability as an example. Are companies intentional at implementing sustainability or are they merely reacting? Are they waiting for external parties like customers or governments to impose rules, or are they taking proactive action? Are they leading the sustainability discussion as trendsetter, or are they merely a follower?

In 2019, the Swedish newspaper *Dagens ETC* decided to be intentional about what advertisements they wanted to see in their newspaper. Believing in a greener and healthier world, they decided to allow only adverts which would support their vision for the future. No more advertisements supporting directly or indirectly the consumption of fossil fuels, so no more ads for weekend trips with air travel, non-electric cars, etc. A bold move. Though the newspaper lost 20% advertisement income, they gained 20% more new individual subscribers. The newspaper also made up for their initial loss with new business customers willing to place green adverts with them.[5]

In February 2019, a ban on advertising food and non-alcoholic drinks with high levels of fat, salt, and sugar came into force across London's Transport for London public transport system. The London authorities took action once they had become aware that child obesity was one of the most ominous health issues facing London. Taking preventive measures in controlling what advertisements were allowed was the right thing to do, and was also a decision that made sense healthwise. A child who is affected by obesity is five times more likely than their healthy weight peers to experience obesity as an adult. It also protects children. Indeed, multiple studies on the effects of advertising on TV and in Internet gaming found that children who were exposed to adverts for unhealthy food consumed more afterwards—both in quantity and calorific load—than those in control groups. In a survey by Cancer Research UK, 40% of respondents aged 11–19 said they felt pressured to eat unhealthily, rising to 52% of people with obesity.[6] Being a nonconformist is about taking a stand.

The preceding examples show that intentional focus is the key to success and happiness. It is also the right thing to do. Permission puts us in the right frame of mind, awareness uncovers the deeper why, and intentionality transforms our insights into choices. Alan Krueger and Daniel Kahneman reported something profound in their research: they found that each of us is an unreliable witness to the realities we are living every day. We distort our recollections of the past: we remember the good as having been better than it was; the bad as being much worse than it was.[7] For example, in Western Europe we don't get much snow in winter. People in my age group and older—so 50 plus—strangely seem to think that "when we were young" we always had snow for Christmas. Looking at the official data for my native Belgium, however, in the last 100 years we only had a white Christmas six times (in 1938, 1950, 1964, 1986, 2009, 2010).

I found a similar delusion in my curiosity research. When asked, over 90% of the people and executives I meet say that their curiosity is above average. These individuals are often stating that they are curious because according to them ... well ... they just are. Or they think they should be, given that curiosity is a desirable trait to have for successful professionals.

Or they do what Daniel Kahneman has called "substitution". He describes substitution as an unconscious cognitive process where people replace a difficult question with a simpler one. So, when we talk about curiosity and inquire whether these executives are curious professionals, these executives substitute my abstract question for an easier one; like, for instance, "Is my self-image that of a competent, intellectual, curious and engaged professional?"[8]

"Big C" versus "Small c" Curiosity

To help deepen the responses to the question: "Are you a curious professional?", I created the concept of "small c" and "big C" curiosity to help people understand the meaning of "substitution" better.

We all have "small c" curiosity. We are born with it—it is a child's magic tool to learn how the world works. Small c curiosity is reactive and as such reacts to external stimuli. It focuses on cues from the world outside. When we get older, this type of curiosity risks becoming shallow and limits itself to exploring the confines of our known world. We say we are curious when prompted because it is socially desirable to say so, not because we are proficient at it.

"Big C" curiosity is intentional and humble, it is not afraid of not knowing. It wants to go deep: both in our known world as well as when exploring new uncharted horizons. Big C curiosity is not afraid to challenge the status quo, even to challenge our biases and limiting beliefs. Big C curiosity wants to explore our inner selves towards deeper self-awareness. Big C curiosity is inherently active. It wants to learn and grow. This is the space of wonder where big idea things are invented and activated. Big C curiosity starts with authentic permission, awareness, and intentionality. Big C curiosity takes more energy, yet provides bigger rewards.

Small c curiosity is about scanning the headlines in a newspaper. Big C curiosity is about reading the actual stories behind the headlines, especially the long complex articles. Small c curiosity is shallow. Small c curiosity asks people how they are doing or how their weekend was, without really being interested in the answer. Big C curiosity is about asking people for deeper insights; for instance, what their biggest highlight of the weekend was, and then waiting for the answer to come.

In his wonderful book *How We Think*, the American philosopher John Dewey explores his version of Big C curiosity with his term "intellectual curiosity", explaining that

---

"in few people, intellectual curiosity is so insatiable that nothing will discourage it, but in most its edge is easily dulled and blunted ... Some lose it in indifference or carelessness; others in frivolous flippancy; many escape these evils only to become encased in a hard dogmatism which is equally fatal to wonder. Some are so taken up with routine as to be inaccessible to new facts and problems."[9]

Which side are you on? All of us have the muscle of a small c curiosity; big C curiosity requires energy.

Strategies to Become Even Better at Intentional Curiosity?

Nurturing your curiosity is essential; it is not a trivial pursuit to be sidelined amidst life's immediate concerns. While health and family take precedence, few things contribute as significantly to your overall well-being as curiosity. Embracing a curious mindset can lead to enhanced personal fulfilment. Allocate time for novel experiences in your schedule, treating it with the same commitment as you would for work or medical appointments. Just as you prioritize those aspects, dedicating time to cultivate your curiosity is crucial. Think of curiosity as a muscle—it flourishes through consistent practice and fades without it. While you are reflecting on these strategies, consider curiosity also as a force for good for collective systems such as teams and organizations.

1. Give Yourself Permission

Permission is where it all begins. Give yourself permission to be curious. This involves acknowledging the value of curiosity and allowing yourself to explore without judgement. Recognize that curiosity is not a distraction but a fundamental aspect of personal and professional growth.

Business angle: Leaders should create an environment where curiosity is encouraged and valued. This can be done by explicitly stating that exploration and questioning are welcome and by rewarding innovative thinking and risk-taking, by inviting minority views to be heard or by designing for creativity and curiosity in the daily job.

2. Slow Down and Observe

Take the time to slow down and observe the world around you and the world inside you. This means being mindful and present in your daily activities, allowing you to notice details and connections you might otherwise miss. Mindfulness can enhance your ability to engage with your curiosity.

Business angle: Encourage teams to take regular breaks and reflect on the past, present, and future. This can improve focus and creativity, leading to more thoughtful and innovative solutions. Train managers and teams in the power of curiosity.

3. Decide Authentically What's Important

Start by deciding what is genuinely important to you and where you want to spend your "curious time". Improving the quality of our lives begins with insights into how we feel about the

(continued)

(continued)

activities that consume our time. Reflecting on what is important allows us to measure and shift the balance of desirable and undesirable actions in our daily lives. Before adding activities that optimize our well-being and removing those that detract from it, we need to understand the motives behind our actions.

Business angle: In a corporate setting, encouraging team members to identify and pursue areas of genuine interest can lead to increased motivation and job satisfaction. Companies can support this by allowing employees to spend a portion of their time on projects or topics they are passionate about, fostering innovation and creativity.

4. Get in the Right Frame of Mind and Maintain Balance

Being in the right frame of mind is often the first spark for creating interest in activities that seem challenging or uninteresting. Set yourself up to respond to rich, exciting moments that capture your attention and open your mind to new possibilities. Achieve this by eating and sleeping well, engaging in mindful meditation, exercising, and investing in your relationships. A balanced state enhances your curiosity and openness to new experiences.

Business angle: Companies can create environments that promote positivity and mental well-being by providing wellness programmes, flexible working hours, and opportunities for social interaction. A positive work environment can lead to increased productivity, creativity, and employee engagement.

5. Apply an Open-Minded and Sceptical Approach

When forming judgements about yourself, others, and the world, always consider alternative perspectives. This mindset is beneficial for various professionals, such as doctors, researchers, journalists, managers, and politicians. Keeping an open mind allows us to discover new possibilities while maintaining healthy scepticism.

Business angle: Helping employees identify and reframe unproductive work habits can lead to improved performance and satisfaction. Encouraging open-mindedness and critical thinking within teams can lead to better decision-making and innovation. Organizations can cultivate this by promoting a culture of questioning, valuing diverse perspectives, and providing training on critical thinking skills.

6. Change Your Script

Changing your script can lead to new and enriching experiences. For instance, next time you are in your favourite coffee shop, instead of replying with a formulaic "How are you" to the barista, go deeper. Say: "Dear (name on nametag), today, I am a 7.2. How are you really today?" and see what happens. Changing your script will change your day.[10]

Business angle: In a business context, a CEO I collaborated with introduced the question: "What are we not seeing in the data?" during business review meetings. He changed the questions and thus changed the depth of his review meetings. This approach encourages deeper thinking and uncovering hidden insights.

7. Create Regular Time and Space for Curiosity

Intentionality means carving out time for curiosity. For instance, Clare Inkster a fellow at the Curiosity Institute created "Curious Thursdays": dedicating one day a week to exploration and new experiences. Use "anchors" (activities that you do routinely, such as brushing your teeth) to remind yourself to be curious about the world, people, and yourself.

Business angle: Companies can foster innovation by allocating regular time for employees to explore new ideas, technologies, or skills. This can be implemented through dedicated innovation days, hackathons, or by encouraging side projects that align with the company's goals.

(continued)

(*continued*)

8. Start Small

Rome was not built in a day and the easiest way to reach this city is by taking the first step towards it. Begin with small steps towards new experiences. Minor adjustments can have a profound impact on your approach to life. Try buying a book from a different section or starting a new curiosity project, like beekeeping and a vegetable garden in my case, to ignite your interest and learning.

Business angle: Encourage teams to experiment with small, incremental changes and pilot projects. This approach minimizes risk and allows for quick learning and adaptation, fostering a culture of continuous improvement and innovation.

9. Surround Yourself with Suitable Guides

Having the right mentors can significantly influence your curiosity. Mentors who understand the uncertainty and emotions of new experiences make exceptional guides. They foster an environment where you perceive new situations as challenges rather than threats, encouraging engagement and creativity.

Business angle: Organizations should invest in mentorship programmes that pair employees with experienced mentors. These relationships can provide guidance, support, and inspiration, helping employees navigate challenges and pursue their curiosity-driven goals.

10. Measure Curiosity

Regularly measure and reflect on your curiosity. Assess the areas where you have grown and identify new areas to explore. Keeping track of your curiosity of the world, in your relationships and of your deeper self, can help you stay committed and recognize the impact it has on your life. Are you interested in measuring your curiosity quotient? I'll be sharing a link at the end of this chapter where you can do this.

Business angle: Companies can implement metrics to measure curiosity and innovation within teams. This could involve measuring curiosity against a maturity scale, tracking the number of new ideas generated, the time spent on exploratory projects, or employee engagement levels. Regular assessments can help maintain a focus on curiosity and its benefits to the organization.

By following these strategies, you can enhance your intentional focus on curiosity, leading to greater personal growth and fulfilment. Implementing these approaches within teams and companies can foster a culture of curiosity, innovation, and continuous improvement, driving both individual and organizational success.

And what about the trigger question we asked at the beginning of the chapter, you might inquire? If you put a frog in cold water and gradually heat up the water, will the frog let itself boil to death? What do you think? Will the frog jump out or get used to the gradually increasing temperature and die? This is a question I often ask in the beginning of corporate keynotes. This metaphor has become engrained in managerial thinking. The story of the frog in boiling water illustrates a metaphor about human nature. If a frog is placed in boiling water, it will immediately jump out to escape. However, if it is placed in tepid water that is gradually heated, the frog fails to perceive the danger and ultimately gets cooked to death. This tale is often used to highlight how people may fail to notice or respond to gradual, incremental threats, compared to sudden, obvious dangers. This metaphor serves as a warning against complacency and the importance of being aware of slow-developing risks. The metaphor of the frog is, however, based on a flawed principle: a frog in cold water that is gradually heated will jump out. Frogs have a superior sensitivity to temperature changes in their environment and react immediately to change. Furthermore, a frog placed into already boiling water will die immediately, not jump out.[11]

Many people get this wrong when I ask the question in presentations. They may have read it in books or heard it from others. I use the metaphor as an example of cognitive laziness. When we receive some information from people in power, like book authors or authorities, we often take what they say for granted without doublechecking facts. Social media influencers, actors, and politicians also wield this power. It pays to be curious and question what others may claim.

Authentic permission, awareness without judging, and driven intentionality are the three steps to create more curiosity in your life. We discussed a number of strategies. Note that we are only getting started with these strategies. There are many more you can embrace. My hope is that you pick a couple which make sense for you. Maybe the next three chapters will help, as we will be taking a deep dive into the different aspects of curiosity. We will be going deep into uncovering the difference between curiosity about the world, about others, and about yourself.

If you want, you can pause here and find out for yourself what your own "curiosity quotient is". To do that, go to https://www.globalcuriosityinstitute.com/individualdiagnostic to take a free curiosity diagnostic survey. It will take you about 12 minutes and in return you'll get a report in your mailbox of your curiosity quotient (score) as well as your curiosity level specific to the three sub-dimensions: world, others, and self. Equipped with your scores, you will enjoy the next chapters a little better. If you want to read the chapters first, then of course, this is fine.

Questions for Reflection

- Reflect on the role of curiosity in finding meaning and satisfaction in life. How can you intentionally integrate more curiosity-driven activities into your routine?
- What are some ideas or projects you've been curious about but haven't pursued?
- What intentional steps can you take to start acting on them?
- How can you cultivate a balance between small "c" curiosity (reactive) and Big "C" curiosity (intentional and deep) in your daily activities?
- How can you foster an environment of intentional curiosity within your team or organization?

Notes

1. eWilleys.com (2020). Zamboni research archives. http://www.ewillys.com/tag/zamboni/
2. Branch, J. (2018). *The 22nd-largest team at the Olympics: Zamboni drivers*. New York, NY: The New York Times.

https://www.nytimes.com/2018/02/19/sports/olympics/
zamboni-drivers-hockey-speedskating-figure-skating.
html (accessed 30 October 2024).

3. Yetto, N. (2023). How the Zamboni Revolutionized Fun
   on the Ice. *Smithsonian Magazine.* https://www.smithso
   nianmag.com/innovation/history-zamboni-revolutionize
   d-fun-ice-180983068/ (accessed 30 October 2024).

4. Kahneman, D., & Krueger, A.B. (2007). Are we having
   more fun yet? *Social Indicators Research* 88 (1):1–30.
   https://www.brookings.edu/wp-content/uploads/2007/
   09/2007b_bpea_krueger.pdf (accessed 30 October 2024).

5. https://www.theguardian.com/environment/2019/sep/26/
   swedish-newspaper-stops-taking-adverts-from-fossil-
   fuel-firms (accessed 25 September 2024).

6. Food Action Cities (2021). *London, United Kingdom: A
   Ban on unhealthy food advertising across the transport
   system.* https://foodactioncities.org/app/uploads/2021/04/
   LCS2_London_Ban_On_Unhealthy_Food_Advertising.
   pdf (accessed 25 September 2024).

7. Kahneman, D., & Krueger, A. B. (2007). Are we having
   more fun yet? *Social Indicators Research* 88 (1):1–30.
   https://www.brookings.edu/wp-content/uploads/
   2007/09/2007b_bpea_krueger.pdf (accessed 30 October
   2024).

8. Daniel Kahneman (2012). *Thinking, Fast and Slow.*
   New York: Penguin.

9. Dewey, J. (1910). *How We Think.* Lexington: D.C. Heath
   & Co.

10. Keohane, J. (2021). *The Power of Strangers: The Benefits
    of Connecting in a Suspicious World.* New York: Random
    House.

11. Gibbons, W. (2007). The legend of the boiling frog is just
    a legend. *Ecoviews.* Savannah River Ecology Laboratory,
    University of Georgia.

Part 3

The Three Dimensions of Curiosity

Curiosity manifests in three dimensions: curiosity about the world (transpersonal curiosity), others (interpersonal curiosity), and self (intrapersonal curiosity). Curiosity about the world bridges the known and unknown, revealing the dual nature of curiosity—interest-driven (I-type) and deprivation-driven (D-type). These types influence personal well-being and professional behaviour, emphasizing curiosity's role in scientific discovery and growth. Curiosity about others fosters deeper relationships and social connections, with genuine, empathetic curiosity enhancing interactions and preventing boredom in long-term relationships. Finally, curiosity about self underscores the importance of self-awareness and introspection. Overcoming self-delusion and biases through continuous learning and feedback from others enhances personal growth. These three dimensions—curiosity about the world, others, and self—collectively drive innovation, improve relationships, and foster personal development. At the system level, when done well, they create high-performing teams and successful organizations.

6

Curiosity About the World Around Us

"Curiosity is the space between the known world and the unknown."

Teddy Frank, Corporate Culture specialist and transformational coach

Trigger Question: how many weeks of curious time on Earth would you say you have in your life?

How much do you know about bees? Bees might be a surprising topic to start this chapter with. In many other areas of our personal and professional lives, there is a tendency to keep things as they are and not explore the new. The old and the known are perceived to provide more stability than the new. Phrases like "I always do it this way" or "This is the way the company expects us to work" might give reassurance; however, when the environment is volatile, sticking to the status quo becomes a hindrance to growth and survival.

Bees have been companions to people for thousands of years. For most of our history, they were the only provider of our sweetener and wax. We have a love-hate relationship with them. While they give us sweet honey, they also sting. My beekeeper coach René van Dormael explained that, until recently, bee colonies were considered to be more valuable than other farm animals, even cows. Stealing a hive would get you five years in prison. Superstition discouraged theft as it was believed that stolen bees would not give their new master honey. Bees were thought of as the favourites of God; unlike wasps, who were believed to be friends of the Devil. Being God's favourites, they were even considered to be intermediaries between this world and the next.

In our journey together throughout the ages, we learned much about these little friends. Yet not all their mysteries were unveiled. Much of their world, their habits, and behaviours remained—and remains—hidden from us. For whatever we did not understand, we created stories. Our minds don't like leaving blanks in our understanding of things. What we don't know, we fill with plausible pieces of pre-existing knowledge. When we see a gap, we try to fill it with something we know already.

In our understanding of bees, a lot of our knowledge was a projection of how we thought they were living, working, and cooperating together. When greater numbers of people begin to believe stories, myths are formed. Myths come before science. Myths start from curiosity as they start with an original need to explain something in the world. However, once a myth becomes accepted, it becomes a rigid story that must not be challenged. Curious inquiry is the crowbar which opens up myths and beliefs through disarming questions. Curious questions can be dangerous and upset the status quo; yet they can also advance collective knowledge and power science.

In this chapter you will explore the first dimension of curiosity: curiosity of the world around us. You can interchange this with intellectual curiosity or transpersonal curiosity. In most societies, this is the most prevalent defining factor of curiosity.

I-Type versus D-Type Curiosity

Why did we start this chapter by talking about bees? Because without these little friends, we would not exist as a species. According to the United Nations Environment Programme, of the 100 crop varieties that provide 90% of the world's food, 71 are pollinated by bees.[1] If bees are so vital in our own food chain, it pays to be curious about them and study their behaviour.

Karl von Frish is probably the most curious bee-researcher that ever lived. A German researcher, he investigated bees and discovered many of the insights we still have now. For instance, he found out that how bees communicate is much more sophisticated than we thought. Bees can communicate through the use of smell, touch, and interestingly also through dance. He found that when a worker bee has found a patch of tasty flowers filled with nectar or pollen, they communicate this through an 8-shaped dance in the hive. The shape of the dance, the speed, duration, even the angle of the turns versus the position of the sun communicate the location, distance, and direction of food sources to fellow worker bees.

Coming to this insight was not easy—it took him years to get there. Try to locate one dancing single bee in a colony of about 50,000 bees in the dark, ever buzzing world of a hive. His curiosity and findings even won him the Nobel Prize in 1973. He had to rely on at least two types of curiosity: "I"-type curiosity and "D"-type curiosity. The I stands for "interest" and the D is an abbreviation for "deprivation". Both types of curiosity have a different origin and are testament to the complex nature of curiosity.

I-type curiosity is activated when individuals recognize opportunities to discover something entirely new; when people develop an intrinsic hunger to learn and are genuinely interested in things. An example of I-type curiosity is the joy we have in reading a book or learning something interesting. Interest-type curiosity gives us a positive feeling, one of joyful exploration. D-type curiosity, on the other hand, is stimulated by a lack of information, and intention to fill a knowledge gap. When we feel deprived of knowledge, we have a desire to eliminate the unpleasant feelings of uncertainty or ignorance. An example is the frustration we have when we don't know something we really want to know; for example, results for a medical examination or a problem we encounter at work that needs to be solved.

People can react to both types of curiosity differently and they can score high or low. If you have taken the curiosity diagnostic of the Curiosity Institute I introduced in Chapter 5, you can find your I-type score under "joyous exploration" and your D-type results under "deprivation sensitivity". I can only imagine that Von Frish scored high on both dimensions. High on I-type curiosity because of the joy he got from years of focus and learning, yet also high on D-type curiosity: science is a hit-and-miss sport. Every time a trial turned out not to producing the results he'd hoped for, he needed to find a new source of energy to motivate himself to keep digging.

In a corporate setting, I-type employees are the constant learners, people who thrive on trying new things. I-type employees find a bigger joy in trying out new gadgets. D-type employees can be different. They are more problem solvers. These are the people who once they have found a problem, put their teeth in it and keep at it until the problem is solved. It is possible for a professional to be high on Interest and low on Deprivation-type curiosity. Different profiles: both very useful to have on your team.

An interesting distinction is that both types have different correlations with well-being. Individuals with I-type intellectual curiosity employ critical thinking as an enjoyable experience, anticipating the pleasure of new discoveries. I-type correlates positively with well-being, as it involves the pleasure of discovery. Individuals with D-type curiosity seek out new information in a desire to eliminate the unpleasant feelings of uncertainty or ignorance. Though people high on D-type deprivation sensitivity curiosity are appreciated as problem solvers ready to go the extra mile and work overtime to solve conundrums, continued high levels of deprivation sensitivity can lead to burnout. D-type curiosity correlates negatively with well-being.

Curiosity about the world is a natural desire to learn new things, understand inner workings, and take a deep dive into subjects that others may find tiresome or burdening. Curious people are those who are not told or asked to learn a topic; they have a persistent need to know and can often be heard asking "why" and probing deeper to learn and understand. Sometimes at their peril.

Curiosity is a mindset, influenced by both our own agency as well as our external environment. Despite the demands of being the President of the United States, Barack Obama dedicated an hour a day to reading while he was in office. Bill Gates reads 50 books a year. Warren Buffett spends 80% of his day reading and acquiring knowledge. Yes, they read because they understand the value of knowledge and its correlation to success. They are not forcing themselves to read; they have a genuine intellectual curiosity and a love of learning that is their central driver. They also created routines which help them with their daily dose of curiosity.

Now why do these habits of Barack, Bill, and Warren impress us? What makes them so different? It cannot be that they are the only ones being curious. After all, we are curious from the moment we wake up to the moment we go to sleep. From dawn to dusk we ask questions, converse with others, look at our social media feeds, listen to music, and consume all kinds of other information. Maybe Barrack,

Bill, and Warren are better at the big C-curiosity we described in the previous chapter?

Bitten by this question, I got curious myself and explored what humanity as a whole is interested in. Given that many use the Internet and Wikipedia, I thought our collective search patterns in a given year (2023) might be a good place to start. Maybe you searched for an answer already. Maybe not. Here is what I found.

What Is Humanity Interested In?

Let's start with the Internet. Of the 10 most visited Internet sites, we mostly visit Google. This is to be expected given it is the first place from which most of us start typing in our questions. The Google homepage is followed by YouTube and then Facebook. We are interested in being entertained by (or learning from) video materials as well as seeing what others in our network are up to. The fourth and fifth most visited sites take us in another direction: Pornhub and XVideos are adult sites. The next five sites are: X, Instagram, Wikipedia, Reddit, and Amazon. At first sight, it seems that our collective curiosity seems to direct us to social media, watch videos, look at erotic images, and buy stuff.

Maybe this is too negative a view. Some questions might go deeper: YouTube and some of these other tools are wonderful for learning all kinds of new stuff and following people that inspire us. Wikipedia is also a tool to satisfy our intellectual hunger.

Diving deeper, what then would be the 10 most visited pages on Wikipedia for 2023? What do you think? Let's have a look: (1) ChatGPT, (2) Deaths in 2023, (3) the 2023 Cricket World Cup, (4) the Indian Premier League, (5) Oppenheimer (film), (6) J. Robert Oppenheimer, (7) Cricket World Cup, (8) Jawan (film), (9) Taylor Swift, and (10) The Last of Us (TV series). In short, we are interested in things that are of immediate interest; like ChatGPT, the lives and deaths of famous people, and sports and entertainment. Unless bees are a hobby, you will likely not want to learn things about them.

Could it be that we're all just too tired living our lives, which compels us to underplay our desire to learn? I'd argue that in the middle of our daily hustle and bustle, being curious helps us grow and expand, if we allow it to happen. In order for us to do so, we need to take the time and create the space to be curious. Intentionality is key. It is easier to slip into a habit of passive entertainment on social media than go for a walk, go to the gym, engage in a deep conversation, or pick up a book to read. Taking action requires more energy than remaining still.

As we have discussed, intentional focus on curiosity helps us survive and keeps us on our toes. The inclination to explore and embrace novelty plays a crucial role in keeping us alert and acquiring knowledge about our ever-evolving surroundings. This might explain why our brains have evolved to release dopamine and other feel-good chemicals in response to encountering new things. Embracing your curiosity is not only an inherent desire but also a path to achievement. Curiosity not only enhances enjoyment and active participation in our work and lives but also contributes to increased learning, engagement, and performance in the workplace. While this concept may seem like common sense, it underscores the idea that being genuinely curious and interested in our activities makes it more natural to become involved, exert effort, and excel.

Where to Start

Where is a good place to start in creating time and space? I'd say pick up a hobby or passion. Any hobby, however small, will give you new wings. It will give you energy, help you ask new questions, and teach you new skills. It will also put you immediately in a learner mindset and help you look at things with new eyes. It's a given that when you start something new, you have permission to suck at it. You can start small or big. Personally, I think you are better off if you don't do it completely on your own, but find like-minded people to learn from and share experiences with.

Engaging in a hobby is a wonderful way to practise curiosity. As you probably have gathered already, I have been exceedingly curious about bees for a couple of years now. In the rural village where we have our country house, a group of local bee-keepers have come together under a wonderful project: to protect the indigenous European black bee

(*Apis Mellifera Mellifera*). While the black bee for long was the only species of honey bee in Europe, other varieties have started to overshadow the black bee to the point where they are at best marginalized, at worst extinct in many regions in Europe.

Starting a new hobby is like experiencing curiosity on steroids. When we start something new, our journey from conscious incompetence to conscious competence is channelled by curiosity. Curiosity makes us ask new questions. When we have no knowledge about something, we cannot be curious about it. If you are a novice at beekeeping, your questions will be pretty basic. Only after gaining initial knowledge will you be able to ask better and deeper questions. And then, after a while, you think of yourself as an expert and curiosity shrinks towards a state where you stop asking questions.

Unless we give ourselves permission, become aware, and take intentional action, this is the trajectory to be expected for new job, a new relationship, a new customer, or a new professional challenge.

This is also true for companies. Start-ups are better at exploration, asking novel questions, and learning from mistakes than scale-ups or grown-up companies. In comparing start-ups and grown-ups, leaders in start-ups profess to be four times more ready to learn from mistakes than leaders in grown-up companies.

Hobbies and passions follow a different path. With passions and hobbies, our curiosity does not settle for the status quo; on the contrary, it remains high and we never tire of going deeper and asking new questions. The reason for this is described in Oliver Burkeman's passionate book *Four Thousand Weeks* on the myth of modern productivity.[2] Burkeman describes hobbies as the ultimate intrinsic motivator, with not the slightest suggestion of external pressure. He shares: "in an age of instrumentalisation, the hobbyist is subversive: he insists that some things are worth doing for themselves alone, despite offering no pay-offs in terms of productivity or profit". He makes the case that in order to be a source of true fulfilment, a good hobby should feel a little embarrassing and that it is fine to be mediocre at them. Without external pressure, our internal flame (curiosity) stays high. Even stronger, without external onlookers, we are ready to be fearless and lean in with curiosity to our anxiety.

Oliver Burkeman also provides an answer to the question I raised at the beginning of this chapter: "how many weeks of curious time do you have on this Earth?" If you live to 80 years of age, you will have enjoyed only 4,000 weeks. With so few weeks available to us, it pays to make the most of them.

Intrinsic and Extrinsic Motivation

Curiosity is an intrinsic force. The Roman statesman and philosopher Cicero described curiosity as follows: "So great is our innate love of learning and of knowledge that no one can doubt that man's nature is strongly attracted to these things even without the lure of any profit."

Those entrepreneurs and intrapreneurs who see their job as an internal source of meaning will also keep their intellectual curiosity high throughout their career. Notice an important aspect to curiosity: it requires time and space. Those individuals, like Barack, Bill, or Warren, carve out time and space to be curious. When they do so, curious professionals like them and many others create a head start for themselves.

If they are surrounded by an organizational culture, leaders, and peers who also create the psychological safety to be curious, magic happens. Leaders who create time and space for the team to be curious are creating the right conditions for high performance teams. Curiosity does not have to be reserved for hobbies.

I have seen curiosity in action in many organizations: for instance, stretched team assignments for the team exploring a new process or technology, project post-mortems to solidify learnings for the future, creating time and space by inviting people to suggest ideas for continuous improvement, innovation hackathons, and many more. What these initiatives have in common is permission to act, awareness that searching for better ways is better than keeping the status quo, and a fearless intentionality to do something about it.

Our journey of understanding curiosity does not, however, end here. Curiosity about the world is just one of three dimensions of curiosity. Eleanor Roosevelt wrote about the importance of being curious in the 24 August 1935, issue of *The Saturday Evening Post*. In her text, she introduces the concept of emotional curiosity as different from intellectual curiosity.

"Perhaps the day will come when our curiosity will not only carry us out of our homes and out of ourselves to a better understanding of material things. But will make us able to understand one another."

Emotions are tools to express our inner being as well as calibrate interpersonal relationships. These two dimensions—curiosity of others and curiosity of self—wait for us in the next chapters.

Questions for Reflection

- Think about a myth or long-held belief in your field. How can you use curious inquiry to challenge and potentially debunk this myth?
- How does your organization currently foster a culture of intellectual curiosity? What practices could be introduced or improved to enhance this culture?

- Reflect on a time when you encountered a knowledge gap. How did you approach filling this gap, and what type of curiosity (I-type or D-type) did you rely on?
- In what ways can you create space in your daily routine to nurture and act on your intellectual curiosity?
- Reflect on a hobby or passion you have. How has this interest contributed to your overall well-being and intellectual growth?

Notes

1. Center for Food Safety (2024). Pollinator protection: impacts on the food supply. https://www.centerforfood safety.org/issues/304/pollinator-protection/impacts-on-the-food-supply (accessed 30 October 2024).
2. Burkeman, Oliver. 4000 Weeks: *Time Management for Mortals*. New York: Farrar, Straus and Giroux, 2021.

7

Curiosity About Others

"The opposite of love is not hate, it is indifference."
Elie Wiesel

"Identifying other people's mistakes and shortcomings is much easier and far more enjoyable than facing your own."
Daniel Kahneman, cognitive scientist,
Nobel Prize laureate

Trigger Question: when you are with others, do you find yourself judging or curious?

Imagine the same situation we explored in Chapter 5: you feel good today. The sun is out, you slept well, and you are ready to face the world with a smile. On your way to work you visit your favourite coffee shop. Unlike other days, you don't have to queue up and you approach the counter. The barista greets you with a smile and says: "How are you?" You look at the nametag on the barista's t-shirt, then look the barista straight in the eye and respond: "Thank you, Alicia, well. Let's see: I'd give it a 7.2 today, how about you?" and then let silence take over. What do you think would happen next?

It takes energy, curiosity, and courage to change the formulaic script of day-to-day interactions. Yet, by doing so, you will have given a gift to people you interact with, like for instance wonderful Alicia. You will have made her feel she matters. Research by Canadian Gillian Sandstrom and Elizabeth Dunn shows that making eye contact feels good and gives us—and Alicia—a happiness boost. They found that connecting with people also makes us more connected to the places in which we live.[1]

In a unique experiment, a group of adults was tasked with striking up a conversation with the barista at their local Starbucks when getting their morning coffee. This request stood out as unconventional, particularly in urban settings where people typically prioritize efficiency in such transactions. Interactions at coffee shops often lean towards minimal communication, with many customers not even making eye contact. However, Sandstrom and Dunn hypothesized that by refraining from engaging with baristas and treating them merely as lifeless service robots, we might be depriving ourselves of something potentially beneficial. The underlying question they sought to explore was whether we could be overlooking a concealed source of belonging and happiness.[2]

This concept represents a fresh perspective in the realm of psychology. Extensive research has indicated that the most significant predictor of happiness and well-being is the quality of a person's social relationships. For instance, an 85-year-long longitudinal Harvard study found that it's not career achievement, money, exercise, or a healthy diet, but positive relationships that keep us happier, healthier, and even make us live longer. According to this research, people who have good relationships are healthier in mind and in body; and people who don't are more susceptible to everything from mental disorders to cardiovascular disease.[3] That alone could spark the idea that it pays to be curious about others.

Maybe our interpersonal curiosity is ready for a reset. In 2023, I was visiting New York to speak at a conference. I arrived the day before and decided I wanted to experience Manhattan. What better way, I thought, than to have dinner in one of the older dining establishments. I normally try out Asian cuisine, but on this occasion, I tried an Italian restaurant around the corner. I was intrigued by one where the interior had retained a pre-Internet feel—tables close to each other and a long eating bar. Many people were sitting alone. None were trying to talk to their neighbour as their companion (their smartphone) was monopolizing their time. I said hi to my neighbour, making a joke that I was a Belgian visiting the city and that nobody speaks these days anymore with strangers. Something magic happened, my neighbour looked at me, put his smartphone away and we started a conversation. Simple, like he was waiting for the invitation. We talked about World War II, that Manhattan (and New York) was primarily Democrat, and many other curious topics.

Speaking to our neighbours is a skill we seem to be losing, especially in big cities. One only has to be on the subway and count the number of people who withdraw into staring at their phones. It is easier to count the ones who don't. I am guilty as charged too, sometimes consuming content that just minutes later I have absolutely no recollection of. Even bumping into someone is not an excuse to make eye contact or start a conversation.

How easy it is to withdraw. Throughout his career studying life in cities, the sociologist Richard Sennett has praised the idea of friction in life: those little inefficiencies that force us to interact with strangers, like asking someone to take picture of you with your smartphone, or asking for directions, or just ordering a meal over the phone. With the march of technological progress, those interactions have become increasingly unnecessary.[4]

And the decreasing interaction in society has eroded our social skills. So much so that US Surgeon General, Dr Vivek Murthy, has described loneliness as an epidemic on par with tobacco use and obesity. He is at the helm of a new World Health Organization Commission to address the hazards of social isolation. In his diagnosis, not only does it undermine physical and mental health, but it also underpins many of our more pernicious ills, including violence, addiction, and extremism. The antidote, he says, is human connection.[5]

Curiosity is the flame to rekindle connection.

To get back to the Starbuck's research mentioned earlier in this chapter, Sandstrom and Dunn took their investigation a step further, questioning whether connections beyond the usual close relationships with family, friends, and co-workers could also contribute positively to our well-being. To explore this, they enlisted 30 men and 30 women for an experiment. Half of the participants were instructed to engage with their baristas, smiling, making eye contact, and engaging in a brief conversation. The other half were directed to make their transaction as efficient as possible. The results revealed that participants who interacted with their baristas reported a heightened sense of belonging, an improved mood, and greater satisfaction with their overall experience.

The study suggests that responding to simple inquiries like "How are you?" with genuine engagement may unlock an additional source of happiness.

The Power of the Curious Conversation

Curiosity has long been associated with intellectual pursuit, engagement with the world, memory, and learning. Yet, as we are starting to discover, curiosity has huge benefits on the interpersonal front too. People who are curious are often viewed in social encounters as more interesting and engaging, they are more apt to reach out to a wider variety of people and have better long-term relationships. In addition, being curious seems to protect people from negative social experiences, like rejection, which could lead to better connection with others over time.

The single fundamental difference between curiosity about the world, which we discussed in

Chapter 6, and curiosity about others is *dialogue*. People talk back, stuff does not. Unlike stuff, we can talk to others and expect a response in return. Of all the management techniques, few are as powerful as curious conversation. If one of your staff tells you how their job is going, or how they think it should change, or what the organization should be doing differently, say "Tell me more" and ask some follow-up questions. It has an instant effect. There may be some initial wariness, especially if people aren't used to having these sorts of interactions with their boss. If you haven't done it, give it a go. It's magic.

Empathetic curiosity can be described as being on a spectrum between shallow and deep. Superficial relationships are formed when we stay shallow and transformative relationships are forged when we allow ourselves to go deep beneath the surface. A lot has to do with your question strategies. Joe Keohane, author of the wonderful book *The Power of Strangers: The Benefits of Connecting in a Suspicious World* advocates us to change our script when we want to go deep, even in mundane situations.[6] His book was the inspiration for the opening story in this chapter.

Curious people have more intense, satisfying social contacts. This is because others perceive curious individuals as more interesting and approachable. What, then, is the difference between polite curiosity versus the nosy overbearing kind? The answer is simple: it all has to do with care. If the communication is held in a mindset of genuine care, there is little danger that the interaction will be construed as nosy. A mindset of care makes you become open to clues and informs you immediately whether your style of communication is being appreciated. In my definition of curiosity, authentically curious people direct their attention to others, not to themselves.

The following phrase by psychology professor Todd Kashdan—"being interested is more important in cultivating and maintaining a relationship than being interesting"—is a testament to this thinking. When we want a relationship to succeed, it is better for the relationship when we approach the connection with an attitude of being interested rather than being interesting. When I talked to him, Kashdan shared: "Curiosity is the secret juice of relationships."[7]

Benefits of Empathic Curiosity

Curious people may also be better at "reading" others. In one study, 96 participants filled out questionnaires rating their own personality traits and how socially curious they were—meaning, how curious they were about how other people think, feel, and behave. Then, they were randomly paired and told to interact for 10 minutes before guessing the personality traits of their partner. Those who were highly curious were able to better predict the extraversion and openness levels of their partners than those who were not very curious, purportedly because they were more accurate in picking up verbal and non-verbal cues. Taken together, these studies suggest that the quality of curiosity can help people to connect better with others, even strangers.[8]

Approaching social interactions with curiosity can significantly improve relationships. The inherent inclination towards novelty associated with curiosity suggests that individuals with a curious mindset may excel at connecting with strangers. In a study done by Kashdan and his academic collaborators, participants engaged in a friendship-building conversation with a trained actor, exploring a series of questions ranging from less to more intimate topics.[9]

Questionnaires assessing curiosity, positive and negative emotion, and social comfort were administered before and after the conversation. Unbeknownst to the participants, actors then rated their attraction and closeness to conversation partners, while participants predicted their own reception. Results indicated that curious participants were more attractive and closer to the actors, and this link between curiosity and intimacy persisted even when considering factors like positive and negative emotion and social anxiety.

In another study, participants were encouraged to converse with unfamiliar peers, and it was found that more curious individuals felt a greater sense of closeness in both situations compared to their less curious counterparts. Demonstrating curiosity through questions and genuine interest fosters a reciprocal exchange, creating a positive spiral of interaction that promotes intimacy.

Remember the trigger question at the start of this chapter: when you are with others, do you find yourself judging or curious? Think of the last meeting you had at work. Reflect on what mental state you were in. Were you finding yourself judging or curious? Judgement is a form of conformity: we judge the other person according to the standards in our head. Curiosity does not compare to what is right or wrong, good or bad. It is open and interested in the other person without judgement. An added bonus is this: curiosity helps us engage more in the meeting.

Curious individuals also cope better with rejection. Research in Japan surveyed 20–39 year olds, measuring overall curiosity, life satisfaction, sensitivity to social rejection, and experiences with social inclusion and exclusion. Curious participants were less likely to experience reductions in life satisfaction or increases in depression even when faced with social rejection, suggesting that curiosity aids in recovering from this potentially devastating experience.

Additionally, curious people exhibit less aggression, as observed in studies measuring responses to emotionally charged situations. Curious participants reported less aggressive responses to hurtful experiences, and in a competitive task involving loud noise blasts, more curious partners were less likely to choose aggressive punishments, particularly in newer relationships. This connection between curiosity and reduced aggression may stem from curiosity's link to perspective-taking, enhancing conflict resolution.

Moreover, curious individuals enjoy socializing more and experience more positive emotions in various social situations. In experiments pairing participants with actors for intimate or casual conversations, those high in curiosity exhibited more positive emotional expressiveness, humour, playfulness, unconventional thinking, and a non-defensive attitude. This suggests that curiosity not only helps recover from negative social experiences but also fosters positive and engaging interactions, even for socially anxious individuals.

I made the case in my earlier book *The Workplace Curiosity Manifesto* that curiosity helps in longer-term romantic relationships, where keeping interest alive is key to preventing break-ups. Dr Arthur Aron has spent decades studying how people develop and maintain close relationships, particularly romantic relationships. He found that most relationships don't end because of conflict or financial difficulty, but because of boredom.[10] Engaging in novel, interesting activities together can be key to making even long-term relationships closer. One of the suggestions I often use is that we can become intentional about reconnecting with our close relationships, like going on a date with our partner of old, creating new joint experiences (even mildly scary ones).

Can empathetic curiosity be cultivated? The aforementioned research findings by Dr Aron indicate that curious individuals contribute positively to social interactions, enhancing the experience, happiness, meaning, and well-being for everyone involved. While curiosity appears to benefit social encounters, the critical question remains: is empathetic curiosity a trait that can be developed, or is it a fixed characteristic? Drawing on the work of Carol Dweck and the positive psychology movement, which has demonstrated the trainability of various positive social traits such as a growth mindset, generosity, compassion, and empathy at all ages, I suggest that curiosity can also be nurtured.[11]

Do try out the following approach in using open-ended questions—ones where the answer is genuinely unknown to the inquirer—and expressing interest, along with follow-up questions. This approach is likely to encourage the respondent to delve deeper, fostering curiosity in both parties. The act of posing open-ended questions can elicit excitement and encourage individuals to reveal more, leading to a natural development of curiosity.

Cultivating interpersonal curiosity can be daunting, especially when interacting with individuals who appear different or intimidating, such as those who are attractive, intelligent, accomplished, or simply "cool". However, avoiding these interactions often leads to more regret than satisfaction. Research shows that our greatest regrets arise not from failing but from not trying at all. Embracing curiosity is key to a fulfilling life. By actively exploring the most intriguing aspects of others, we can deepen our relationships, ultimately enhancing our happiness and success.

We can encourage social curiosity in our corporate setting. I shared the concept of "never eat alone at work" during a company-wide presentation for the Danish Diary company Arla, after which the Human Resources team took this comment to heart. They decided to reserve two "curiosity tables" in their cafeteria. Colourful place mats are placed on the tables reading: "Feed your curiosity." If you are eating alone, chances are you will find a welcoming curious crowd at the table ready to engage in a conversation.

A Better Question

Are you ready for a quick, curious exercise? One question I suggest you ask today is the following: "What can I do to be a better ..." (fill in your relationship with the other person: it can be partner, colleague, customer, boss, son, daughter, neighbour, or any other relationship you may have). You might experience this question as vulnerability as much as curiosity. I guarantee that you will not only learn something: your relationship will become better because of this question.

Why, then, does asking a simple question like this feel daunting to most of us?

According to Tasha Eurich, the self-awareness researcher we met earlier, "asking for feedback makes us uncomfortable, we prefer to find ways to justify our willful ignorance".[12]

Still, try it; put on your cloak of humility and try it out. I promise you that the feedback will help you grow more than sticking your head in the sand like an ostrich.

The world of curiosity as we know it narrowly in our day-to-day language is expanding as we progress through this book. We covered curiosity about "stuff" in the last chapter. This chapter has been all about how we can create better relationships with the empathic side of curiosity. Curiosity in both these cases relies heavily on our visual capabilities. We need to see and look at "stuff" or people in order to be triggered into curiosity. Yet what happens when we don't have eyes to see or when we are curious about an area where visuals don't help? This is the hardest dimension yet, I will argue, the most rewarding one. In the next chapter, we will discuss what happens when we become curious about our deeper selves, our purpose, our beliefs, even our limiting beliefs and our biases.

Questions for Reflection

- How do you currently handle feedback and criticism from others? Could approaching these interactions with more curiosity improve your response and growth?

- Reflect on a recent meeting. Did you find yourself judging others or being curious about their perspectives? How did this impact the outcome of the meeting?

- In what ways can you incorporate more curious conversations with open-ended questions into your daily work routine? What specific actions can you take?

- Reflect on the quote by Todd Kashdan: "Being interested is more important in cultivating and maintaining a relationship than being interesting." How can you apply this principle in your interactions with colleagues, clients, and other stakeholders?

- How do you typically respond to the question, "How are you?" How might your interactions change if you responded more thoughtfully?

Notes

1. Sandstrom, G.M. and Dunn, E.W. (2014). Social interactions and well-being: The surprising power of weak ties. *Personality and Social Psychology Bulletin* 40 (7): 910–922. doi: 10.1177/0146167214529799

2. Ibid.

3. Mineo, L. (2017). *Harvard Study, Almost 80 Years Old, Has Proved That Embracing Community Helps Us Live Longer, and Be Happier.* Cambridge: *The Harvard Gazette.* https://news.harvard.edu/gazette/story/2017/04/over-nearly-80-years-harvard-study-has-been-showing-how-to-live-a-healthy-and-happy-life/ (accessed 30 October 2024).

4. Sennett, R. (2012). *Together: The Rituals, Pleasures, and Politics of Cooperation.* New Haven: Yale University Press.

5. Rowland, K. (2024). US surgeon general Vivek Murthy: 'Loneliness is like hunger, a signal we're lacking something for survival'. New York: *The Guardian.* https://www.theguardian.com/lifeandstyle/2024/jan/29/us-surgeon-general-vivek-murthy-loneliness-mental-health-epidemic-social-media#:~:text=US%20surgeon%20general%20Vivek%20Murthy,re%20lacking%20something%20for%20survival (accessed 30 October 2024).

6. Keohane, J. (2021). *The Power of Strangers: The Benefits of Connecting in a Suspicious World.* New York: Random House.

7. Kashdan, T.B. (2009). *Curious? Discover the Missing Ingredient to a Fulfilling Life.* New York: William Morrow & Co.

8. Suttie, J. (21 May 2017). Why curious people have better relationships. *Greater Good Magazine.* https://greatergood.berkeley.edu/article/item/why_curious_people_have_better_relationships (accessed 30 October 2024).

9. Kashdan, T.B. and Roberts, J.E. (2004). Trait and state curiosity in the genesis of intimacy: Differentiation from related constructs. *Journal of Social and Clinical Psychology* 23: 792–816. doi: 10.1521/jscp.23.6.792.54800

10. American Psychological Association (2022). *Speaking of Psychology: What Makes Love Last? With Arthur Aron, PhD.* Washington: American Psychological Association. https://www.apa.org/news/podcasts/speaking-of-psychol

ogy/lasting-love#:~:text=Aron%20has%20spent%20dec
ades%20studying,is%20our%20own%20personal%20
growth (accessed 30 October 2024).

11. Dweck, C.S. (2006). *Mindset: The New Psychology of Success*. New York: Random House.

12. Eurich, T (2017). *Insight: The Surprising Truth About How Others See Us, How We See Ourselves, and Why the Answers Matter More Than We Think*. New York: Crown Currency.

8

Curiosity About Self

"The two most important days in your life are the day you are born and the day you find out why."
Mark Twain, writer

"I am on my way to being who I am, as opposed to having lived who I thought I should be."
Henry Winkler, actor

Trigger Question: is it possible that when breathing, your flow of air alternates between your right and left nostril?

If you were to ask an incarcerated person how they compare to non-incarcerated individuals, would they say they have committed more criminal behaviour than you or I? How would you guess this person would compare themselves to a "normal" person on categories like being law-abiding, trustworthy, and honest?

Chances are that you are in for a curious surprise. Psychology professor Constantine Sedikides asked prisoners in the United Kingdom this very question. He gave the prisoners—many of whom had committed brutal crimes—a list of nine positive personality traits and asked them to rate themselves on each in comparison to two groups: other prisoners and non-inmate community members. The traits were: moral, kind to others, trustworthy, honest, dependable, compassionate, generous, self-controlled, and, finally, law abiding. The results he got back from inmates were not really what he was hoping for. How do you think the criminals responded?

These prisoners rated themselves superior to their fellow inmates on all measures. When they compared themselves to normal citizens, they even thought themselves not to be equal, but superior in eight of the nine dimensions. The one exception? According to Sedikides, inexplicably: "they rated themselves as equally law-abiding compared to community members."[1]

Delusion is not unique to inmates; we all suffer from it. It is hard for people to see past the delusional stories we tell ourselves. For every 10 people who say they are self-aware, there is only a single one who actually is. Behavioural economist and Nobel Prize laureate Daniel Kahneman has tapped into a profound truth when he observes that humans have an "almost unlimited ability to ignore our ignorance".

Indeed, studies indicate that we often believe we are smarter, funnier, leaner, more attractive, more socially adept, more athletically talented, superior students, and better drivers than objective measures would suggest. Researchers refer to this phenomenon as the "Better Than Average Effect". It is easy for us to recognize the problems in others, yet we fail to see the proverbial plank in our own eyes. We have two eyes to look at the world and at others; we don't have the same tools to observe our own selves properly.

In this chapter, we will focus on the power of intrapersonal curiosity, exploring what happens when we give permission to question our hard held believes, become aware of our biases, and use this new insight to take intentional action to become a better version of ourselves.

Why It Is Hard to Explore Our Deeper Self

I recently was talking to Jelle Zeeboer, a personal trainer in the Netherlands. He guides people to live a healthier life. He focuses on physical fitness, yet takes pride in also talking about food and mental matters to ensure his customers get the most out of their investment. His customers pay several hundred euros every month, meaning they are well-off middle-class citizens looking to do better. Jelle told me that he is surprised every time these folks show that they are unaware of the benefits or detriments of their food intake. They don't know the nutritional value of the food they eat. Yet, if you were to ask these people whether they are good at self-reflection and are self-aware citizens, they will likely answer in the affirmative.

According to an old legend, there was once a time when all human beings were equal to God, but they so abused their divinity that God decided to take away their most important ability—self-awareness—and hide it in a place where it could never be found. To find the best spot, he held a council of his advisors to help him decide. "Let's bury it deep in the earth," said one advisor. God answered, "No, that will not do, because humans will dig into the earth and find it."

Another advisor replied, "Okay, let's sink it in the deepest ocean then." But God said, "No, not there, for they will learn to dive, and they will find it." Then a third advisor said, "What about the highest mountain top, out in the farthest corner of the earth?"

But again, God replied, "No, that will not do either, because they will eventually climb every mountain, scale every peak, search every hidden cave and once again find and take up their divinity."

The advisors were exasperated. They threw up their arms in surrender. "There is no place!" they hollered. "The humans will proliferate, and they will find it anywhere we put it."

God was quiet for a time. He thought long and deep. Finally, he looked up at his advisors, a knowing twinkle in his eye. "Here is what we shall do," he said. "We will hide their self-awareness deep down in the one place they will surely never look—the very centre of their own being." All rejoiced. Of course! It was the perfect place! They all formally agreed on it, and the deed was done.

Ages passed, and since that time, humans have been on a desperate and unending search, travelling every corner of the planet, digging, diving, climbing, and exploring—searching for the one thing they know they've lost, and just can't seem to find. Only with curiosity can we become more self-reflective and self-aware.

Now, self-reflection is key to understanding ourselves better; it is not just "thinking about ourselves". We have seen already in this chapter that we have an incredible capacity to create erroneous stories about ourselves. We easily believe things that prove not to be right. There is a telling quote attributed to Mark Twain that highlights this well:

> "It ain't what you don't know that gets you into trouble. It's what you know for sure that just ain't so."

It is not that introspection does not work, it's that many people are assuming that they know how to do it, but in fact are doing it wrong. Trying to understand your feelings and beliefs requires that you hone your intuition, lean in with humility, become aware of your biases, and create time and space for introspection.

It seems that a number of people think they are untouched by biases. So much so that there is even bias called "I am not biased"-bias: it is the belief that other people have biases, but that you are rational and immune to them. The smarter you are, the higher you score on an IQ test, or the more successful you are, the more likely you are to fall victim to the "I am not biased"-bias and thus the worse you are in recognizing your own limitations.[2]

This seems to be also more likely true for senior leaders. Research shows that the more successful executives are, the more they overestimate their skills. Compared to front line leaders and middle managers, senior executives overvalue their empathy, adaptability, coaching, collaboration, and also ... self-awareness skills.[3] If you are a leader, curiosity is your biggest ally for success. Compared to less curious peers, curious leaders are better at operational efficiency, continuous improvement, innovation, and are also more respected and command more engagement and productivity in the teams they lead.

Intelligence is the ability to think and learn; wisdom is the quality of your judgement.

Forget about executives: what about parents? Research shows that the majority of mothers and fathers grossly overestimate the number of words they speak to their children.[4] We think we are more communicative with our young children than we really are.

Stages of Self-reflection

Self-reflection follows three stages. First of all, we need to allow it, give ourselves permission to slow down and reflect. Second, we pause and become aware of ourselves, the deeper reasons why we do the things we do, say the things we say and think the things we think. We can do this alone or more easily with the help of a coach or therapist. This second stage will provide us with the wisdom to learn more about ourselves, our purpose, our values, deeper drivers, underlying (even limiting) beliefs and biases. The final stage, then, is the stage of insight where we decide how to get better at those areas we want to improve on. This is also the stage where we action our insights and create a new daily habits and routines.

In my keynotes, I always want to spark people's surprise. When I am able to surprise people and throw them off guard, they open up more to what I will tell them. Trivia quizzes are great for this, especially if the question is slightly "off". For instance, ask people: true or false—you alternate sides of your nose when breathing. At times you inhale/exhale on the right side and at other times you do the same from your left nostril. If you are in agreement with my statement, raise your arm. If you think this is not true, don't do anything. Most of the time, very few arms go up. The answer to this question that I propose seems to be way off. To liven up the room, I sometimes invite people to raise both arms if they think my claim is utterly preposterous. Laughter follows then with a number of people just doing this: raising both arms in confidence. When looking at people's faces, they shine with confidence, as if they are saying to themselves: "This cannot be true. I know, I am the one breathing. I know myself best."

Later in the presentation, I share with them that they have it all wrong. We do in fact breathe through one dominant nostril at a time. Every 40 minutes or so, our breathing changes sides. Our body does this to calibrate right and left brain hemispheres. I have had many medically trained people, including doctors and surgeons in my presentations, who are oblivious of this fun fact. This fact about breathing is not something they learned in medical school. If you are into yoga and breathwork, this is common knowledge. I use this example of breathing to make a point about how ignorant we can be at times of things staring us in the face. We breathe all the time, yet we are completely oblivious to the mechanics of it. Not knowing the answer, we assume we know the answer and are ready to defend it, even raising both arms to disqualify the question. I then continue to say: "How many other things in life we are confident about could be eluding us, or plainly wrong?"

When we hear something that does not correspond with our own perception of how things work, we gladly push it away and discredit it. This is a function of conformist thinking. Our beliefs are a part of who we are. Information that goes against them threatens the core of our personality. We resist that. We don't want to question our beliefs and who we are. Toddlers believe their parents when they say they saw a small elephant with long ears flying through the air because, for toddlers, the world is still entirely new. They often notice that very strange things can indeed be possible.

But adults have strong beliefs that are not easily shaken. And in many cases, that is justified. Often, we are right. The sun rises and sets, gravity exists, our toothpaste still tastes the same, and there are no flying or pink elephants. This makes it very difficult to change unfounded beliefs or to allow new ideas. If new ideas risk rocking our boat, we stay away from them. In those moments, we are not curious. Quite the contrary.

When you are asked a new question, or when you are presented with a novel idea, you must think about the answer. At that moment, you are invited, challenged even, to reconsider your current position, to rephrase it, or to admit that you simply see it incorrectly. You are invited to train yourself in mental agility. You must be willing to let go of your own perceived truth to make room for objectivity. This is hard, yet it happens even if our thoughts or beliefs are wrong. Or outdated. Ignorance is perceived as weakness. God forbid we appear as not knowing, not in control.

Three Types of Blind Spots

According to Tasha Eurich,[5] whom we met earlier, there are three types of blind spots: knowledge blind spots, emotion blind spots, and behaviour blind spots. Blind spots are a good way to describe our barriers to curiosity of self.

Knowledge blind spots are grounded in the illusion that we think we are more knowledgeable than we actually are. The fact that you are a rational being in a certain body gives

(continued)

(*continued*)

you the false confidence that you know the workings of (at least simple) processes like flow of air breathing. The more experience we think we have, the surer of ourselves we are. In our example, the more unlikely I think the answer is to the question of breathing, the more sure I am that I'm right. It takes lots of humility to consider that I am wrong and curiosity to open up to things I don't know.

Emotional blind spot is a term that describes the fact that, even without realizing it, we often take decisions less from place of rationality and more from a place driven by emotions.

The third blind spot—behaviour blind spots—refers to the fact that we have trouble in looking at ourselves in the third person.

I have found a good strategy to overcome my own blind spots. When I catch myself in a state of hubris and overconfidence, I try to identify my deeper assumptions about the situation or the person. This may sound obvious, but unfortunately, as we have seen, it is hard and rare to question our assumptions about ourselves and the world around us, especially for ambitious, successful, and self-confident people. For instance, when you next fail at something, check your assumptions about what failure means to you. In my own case: I was imprinted early on that failure meant that I might not be a good boy. And only good boys deserve appreciation and love.

I encourage you to try it. Also observe your reaction to the situation: do you blame yourself or try to cast blame for failure onto others? Most people blame others: the Harvard psychologist Chris Agyris found that when something does not go the way we want or expect, we typically assume that the cause is external to ourselves.[6]

Another strategy is remarkably simple. When we are in a good mood, we are more interested in whatever grabs our attention, and we see the world around us with inquisitive eyes, discovering that much of what surrounds us is more captivating than we thought. Being in a good mood simply means we are healthy in mind and body. We feel in balance physically, mentally, socially, and spiritually.

When in a positive state, we are more likely to avoid hastily committing to ideas and judgements. Embrace the idea that there is always an alternative perspective, and there is probably something receiving excessive attention while something intriguing remains overlooked. A good way to get there is to eat and sleep well, engage in daily rituals of mindful meditation and exercise, and make a daily effort to invest in your relationships.

The first step towards self-reflection is realizing that it is important. That a time-out, however short, is a good thing to do. That whatever we find through this process is OK, even when it goes against our current beliefs. That if we open ourselves to new learning, we grow as a person. Or as a team, because self-reflection can also be practised in a group setting. I find it remarkable that we are so good at doing things in teams, but when it comes to challenging the status quo or reflecting on why we do the things we do, we suddenly don't take the time. Take post-mortems or after-action reviews. I have come across few companies who do this well: take the time to learn from mistakes (e.g., why we lost a customer deal), are honest enough to articulate the root causes beyond platitudes, are ready to internalize them (and not blame competition or the customer) and face the facts courageously, and then take the necessary action to mitigate.

The Lost Art of Introspection

The question about breathing raised at the start of this chapter and again a little later hides another issue; namely, that we have been trained to be rational animals, not feeling agents in tune with our intuition and what our bodies tell us. In our rational society, we are more aware of our thinking processes than what happens at the physical level. Many people have forgotten how to feel, how to listen to their bodies, how to tune into their intuition. When did you last listen to the clues your breath is giving you?

Next time you are feeling good, observe your breath and notice how it flows: in and out. Is it longer going in versus going out? Is it the same? Is it calm? Then observe how you breathe when something happens: someone doing something dangerous on the road in front of you, when you enter the room with your boss for a salary raise discussion. Knowing your breath will allow you to master it. Navy Seals learn to use their breath to prepare for high intensity missions. They practise "block breathing". We can all benefit from it. In equal measures of four slow counts of nose breathing, you breath in four counts, hold your breath for four counts, breath out slowly in four counts, and hold again for four counts. Do this several times. Like Navy Seals, this will help you focus on your job interview or on your important customer presentation.

There are many other breathing techniques. My partner uses many of them in her psychotherapy sessions with clients. For instance: "the humming bee breath". This one is excellent to help us unwind. The technique is simple: you breathe out longer than you breathe in. When you breathe out through your nose, make a humming sound. For extra effect, you can put your hands on your ears. Our body is such a wonderful machine, if we only take advantage of it.

Stop for a moment, close your eyes and zoom in on your body. Do you notice anything in general or specific about your breath? Or do you notice any sensations you did not when your eyes were open? This is the first step to using embodied curiosity to help you step into your intuition. Now think of a happy situation and see what happens to your body. How does your body react, which areas light up, do you sense a tightening or untightening of certain muscles? Take your time to fully observe. How easy is this for you?

Many have lost the capacity to listen to their bodies. This capacity is called *interospection* by specialists. It is the process by which we sense, interpret, and then integrate signals from within our body. Maybe you might want to also consider a less happy situation and again observe—feel what is happening. If you are good at this first step: great. If you struggle: no worries, it means that you have not trained your muscle of introspection much. If you feel nothing, you are not abnormal: you are like many people.

However, research shows that if we keep this skill underdeveloped, it could backfire. According to an article in the *Biological Psychiatry: Cognitive Neuroscience and Neuroimaging* journal of June 2018,[7] "Dysfunction of interoception is increasingly recognized as an important component of different mental health conditions, including anxiety disorders, mood disorders, eating disorders, addictive disorders and somatic symptom disorders [sleep disorders]." The good thing is that with dedicated effort, you can develop this skill and tune in more to your intuition.

Introspection is a practice. With regular and continuous practice over time, we get better at it. Practices like yoga and mindfulness have been found to help us hone our capacity for deeper observation of ourselves. I am a regular meditator and have become generally more peaceful, more grounded, more balanced in my interactions with the world. During those periods when I meditate daily, I also find myself able to focus better and for longer periods at work. The hard thing is finding the time. Meditation is important but not urgent, hence it often slips from the to-do list. For me, early morning works best.

I have not tried the museum exercise yet (the one we looked at earlier, when you are required to look at one painting for three hours), but I have tried something similar. Every year, I give myself a gift. I join a 10-day Buddhist silence meditation, called vipassana by the in-crowd. Ten hours of meditation every day, eyes closed, not talking to others, even no eye contact. Also, no books or smartphones. Not even a pen to write things down with. Becoming aware is harder than you think.

Personally, day three and day six are always the hardest and those days I often ask why on Earth I am torturing myself. Why not quit and go back to normal life? Still, I persevere, because I know that I need the time off in silence to pay attention and to get in a new zone. One where I start looking at myself with new eyes. Every time I learn so much about myself, things which would remain hidden otherwise.

The technique you follow is simple: you are invited to focus on yourself, to observe your breath, and everything that happens in your body. Easy, right?

I promise you it is not—there are two challenges. First of all, detailed observation is difficult. It is easy to observe ourselves superficially, then take a confident assessment of what's wrong. We are after all better at action. Try to observe the tip of your nose or the area beneath it, or your little toe. Beginners in vipassana are invited to spend the first three days observing the area beneath the nose. When we are good at details, it is easy to zoom out. The problem is that zooming out, like most of us are used to, misses granularity and might lead us to jump to conclusions or even delude ourselves into believing that we know the answer.

Another challenge is time. To observe oneself for 30 seconds is easy, try it for three minutes and you find that you are distracted and thinking of your to-do list or wondering what's for lunch. Focusing is hard. And yet, if we stick with it, magic happens. Every time I do a vipassana, I come out with deep new insights about myself and am more in tune with my intuition.

Continuous Learning

Even though we have not called it out specifically, *continuous learning* is a key strategy to become better at self-reflection. The more we learn, the more we fill our database with new information. The more angles of a problem we understand, the more we can reflect on it objectively and avoid explanations or decisions based on overconfidence or emotions. Learning can be done both in areas where we already know a lot as well as in areas where we are novices. I describe the distinction between both by using the terms *deep curiosity* and *broad curiosity*.

Going deep with curiosity helps us to go deeper in areas where we already have expertise. We need to keep learning not only to deepen our knowledge, but to keep us in the zone of wonder and out of the zone of overconfidence. Learning keeps us on our toes in the world we know, and also helps us to discover new territories.

There is a distinct social dimension to self-reflection. On the one hand, when we are good at observing ourselves, we can also develop a better intuition of others, the people we live and work with, and get better at observing the emotions and reactions of the people we interact with. On the other hand, we get better at self-reflection when we seek feedback on our abilities and behaviours. People around us, colleagues, family members, coaches, or mentors can almost always see what we can't and therefore we need to surround ourselves with those who will tell the truth. We need people who will lovingly bring us back on track when we derail.

Leaders, too, have the capacity to make the people they touch grow, and motivate their team to become a better version of itself. We will discuss curious leader behaviour in the chapter 10. Clearly, leaders are key in orchestrating a sense of curiosity in the workplace and can encourage employees to reflect on their work, question assumptions, and seek innovative solutions.

Let's make things even more real. In the next couple of chapters, we will be diving together into practical applications of curiosity. In the next chapter, we will be exploring the power of better and curious questions.

Questions for Reflection

- What kind of impact does your behaviour have on other people, when you get triggered, and how do they react?
- What kind of situations or other people's behaviour trigger negative emotions and reactions in yourself?
- What are some common biases or assumptions you hold about yourself? How do these impact your decision-making and interactions with others?
- How do you typically react to feedback about your behaviour or performance? What does this reaction reveal about your self-awareness?
- Is reflection encouraged in your organization? Is there time to balance "thinking" with "doing"? For instance, after each project, is there sufficient time put aside to reflect on what went well and what could be done better.

Notes

1. Eurich, T. (2017). *Insight: The Surprising Truth About How Others See Us, How We See Ourselves, and Why the Answers Matter More Than We Think*. New York: Crown Currency.
2. Pronin, E., Lin, D.Y. and Ross, L. (2002). The bias blind spot: Perceptions of bias in self versus others. *Personality and Social Psychology Bulletin* 28(3): 369–381. doi: 10.1177/0146167202286008
3. Eurich, T. (2017). *Insight: The Surprising Truth About How Others See Us, How We See Ourselves, and Why the Answers Matter More Than We Think*. New York: Crown Currency.
4. Hart, B. and Risley, T.R. (1995). *Meaningful Differences in the Everyday Experience of Young American Children*. Towson: Paul H Brookes Pub Co.
5. Eurich, T. (2017). *Insight: The Surprising Truth About How Others See Us, How We See Ourselves, and Why the Answers Matter More Than We Think*. New York: Crown Currency.
6. Argyris, C. (May 1991). Teaching smart people how to learn. *Harvard Business Review Press*. https://hbr.org/1991/05/teaching-smart-people-how-to-learn
7. Khalsa, S.S., Adolphs, R., Cameron, O.G. et al. (2018). Interoception and mental health: A roadmap. *Biological Psychiatry: Cognitive Neuroscience and Neuroimaging* 3 (6): 501–513. https://www.sciencedirect.com/science/article/pii/S2451902217302343 (accessed 31 October 2024).

Part 4

Applying Curiosity

This part of the book explores the practical application of curiosity in a number of important areas. We emphasize the transformative power of curiosity in personal, professional, and societal contexts. Chapter 9 explores the benefits of asking better questions, using examples like the Titanic disaster to illustrate the dangers of overconfidence. Chapter 10 highlights the importance of curiosity in leadership, using unconventional approaches to improve performance and innovation. Chapter 11 discusses the role of curiosity in integrating AI and technology, balancing efficiency with critical thinking. Chapter 12 examines how curiosity fosters thriving workplace cultures, enhancing innovation, engagement, and inclusivity. This chapter focuses on corporate values, emphasizing curiosity's role in driving positive transformation. Finally, Chapter 13 delves into the impact of curiosity on environmental sustainability, advocating for behaviour change and innovative solutions to global challenges. Across these chapters, curiosity is presented as a vital force for growth, creativity, and adaptation in an ever-changing world.

9

"Why Don't We Milk Pigs" or: The Power of Better Questions

"Questions are places in your mind where answers fit. If you haven't asked the question, the answer has nowhere to go."

Clay Christensen

Trigger Question: how many questions did you ask as a child? And how many questions do you ask now?

What questions did you ask yourself this morning when waking up? Did you ask deep existential questions, or rather simple questions to start your day? Were these questions about the world, your relationships, or about yourself? Did you ask questions at all?

A failure to ask questions is the root cause of many disasters. The sinking of the Titanic was not due to the presence of icebergs, but because the crew of the Titanic did not do anything with the reports of nearby icebergs they received from nearby ships.[1] The crew was so overconfident of the might of their ship that they did not bother to ask for more information. A failure to ask new questions also prevents us from growing.

The Benefits of Curiosity

Think about when you were really positively curious about something. How did you feel? Exploring curiosity triggers the release of dopamine and provides a boost of energy. Consistent practice is linked to enhanced job performance, a heightened sense of purpose, elevated levels of life satisfaction, improved mood, and increased perseverance and grit. The cultivation of curiosity facilitates the learning process and improves memory storage. Venturing into new experiences and seeking fresh information not only builds self-efficacy but also fosters resilience to future stressors.

Interpersonal curiosity extends its positive impact to social aspects as well. Individuals with a curious mindset tend to exhibit traits such as open-mindedness, playfulness, creativity, and emotional expressiveness. Research indicates that they possess greater tolerance for anxiety and uncertainty, displaying less defensiveness, aggression, or judgement towards others.[2]

Developing curiosity serves to strengthen relationships and learning, and also strengthens our understanding of ourselves. Curiosity enables us to go inward and engage in self-reflection. This helps us to become aware of our assumptions and biases, approaching situations with an open mind.

Growing Up

"Every child is an artist, the problem is remaining an artist when we grow up" is a quote attributed to Pablo Picasso. The sentiment of the quote aligns well with Picasso's views on creativity and the importance of retaining a childlike sense of wonder and imagination. The same sentiment is shared by Steve Jobs's advice to Stanford students: "Stay hungry, stay foolish."

Is there a difference between the curiosity of kids and that of adults, and what can we learn from it?

"How many questions do kids ask between the ages of 4 and 6 on a daily basis?" is a question I often ask when addressing audiences. The numbers people throw at me range from 40 to 1 million. In such cases, I point out that a day only has 86,400 seconds, and that "1 million" questions is probably a metaphor for "too many".

I often share the research done by Sam Wass. He studied a group of 1,500 parents and children between the ages of three and five, and calculated the average number of questions children asked to be 73 per day.[3]

Now, do the number of questions asked by children decrease when they start going to school, you may ask. Though schools have their role in decreasing the curiosity of children, the reality is that after the age of five the novelty seeking kind of curiosity decreases regardless of the influence of schools. The moment children start to make sense of the world and accept how things are structured, they turn their seeking behaviour elsewhere.[4]

The type of questions children ask vary. What these questions have in common is that they help children to make sense of the world around them and they are not limited by preset beliefs. Children are perfectly fine to ask questions like: "Why don't we milk pigs?" This was a real question the scientist and educationalist Nathan Isaacs heard a young girl ask her mother. The answer "Because they have little ones of their own to feed" did not, however, satisfy her, as she followed up with: "So do cows have calves ...". Young children are capable of pursuing knowledge with penetrating, remorseless logic.[5] In fact, this fearlessness is the biggest difference between adults and children.

Against popular belief, we adults are also curious. We ask many questions out loud or in our head. The difference from our younger friends is that we are most often not ready to take risks in the pursuit of answers to our questions. We don't pursue the question because we think we know the answer, or we are afraid of an answer we might not like, that not knowing might make us look less in the eyes of others, or we are overwhelmed with stress. Stress stifles curiosity.

Children don't have these qualms. They are perfectly willing to put their tiny fingers in a lit match, just to experience the feeling of heat. When, however, these young children grow up and reach adolescence, we see a drop in the number of questions they ask. From the 73 questions they used to ask as children, the number of questions adolescents ask runs in the single digits. The once fearless and many childhood questions have been replaced with more practical and fewer questions. One finding shows that the number of questions asked has a social connection: the number of questions the adolescent asks has a direct correlation with how cool it is in the tribe—that is, family and peer group—to ask questions.

Once these youngsters follow their normal trajectory into the workforce, their questions become functional. The wide and broad childhood questions have made room for questions such as: "How do I fit in", "How do I stay out of trouble", "How do I please my boss."[6] That's at least the trend for most professionals.

Some remain excessively curious throughout their lives. And these individuals are the heroes of the corporate world, especially in knowledge intensive environments. There is not a single senior executive who does not value what curious professionals bring. For instance, the founder of Dell, Michael Dell, claims that:

"There is no better catalyst to success than curiosity."

Michael Dell's view underscores curiosity as an essential trait for leaders and innovators, enabling them to navigate challenges, drive progress, and create lasting impact. Indeed, when I ask in my surveys what differentiates curious professionals from their less curious peers, the answer that comes out on top is: curious professionals are more ready to turn ideas into action. Curiosity is action driven. And the best ideas are fed by the best initial questions.

Four Reasons We Don't Ask Questions

Questions are the way in which curiosity makes itself heard. When we are curious, we ask questions like "why, what if, how". These questions can be in our mind or expressed to others. As we all know, it can be hard to ask questions at times, let alone ask good questions. How often do you walk away from an encounter and think: "I wish I'd asked that question?" While we are all born with the capacity to ask questions, our ability to do so is unequally distributed.

Professor Michael J. Marquardt identifies four reasons that we don't ask questions when we ought to:[7]

- Because of a desire to protect ourselves from the danger of looking stupid.
- Because we are too busy.
- Because the culture discourages questions.
- Because we lack the skills required to ask them.

We explore each of these dimensions in the following sections.

Because of a Desire to Protect Ourselves from the Danger of Looking Stupid

As adults, when we are very knowledgeable about a certain topic, we are confident, sometimes even fearless in asking questions when engaging in a discussion with a person we perceive to be at par or less knowledgeable than ourselves. When, on the other

hand, we are in the company of people with superior knowledge, or even worse, we are in a group
setting, we risk feeling overwhelmed and refrain
from asking questions, even the life-saving ones.

I referenced the reason the Titanic sank—
because of the lack of questions on the part of the
crew. After the tragedy, people involved in the con-
struction of the Titanic admitted that they had had
questions about the ship's safety that they did not
raise in front of colleagues or bosses, for fear of
appearing foolish.[8]

Fitting in versus challenging the status quo can
be a powerful force against asking questions. Even
in senior management teams, the desire to fit in with
the group can be stronger than the desire to raise a
potentially damaging question.

Because We Are Too Busy

A little bit of stress forces us out of our comfort zone
and is actually good for our growth and development. We need a nudge lest we remain in the status
quo forever. Too much stress, on the other hand, and
curiosity takes a nose-dive. In high-pressure work
environments, people prefer to focus on the task at
hand rather rethink the process or customer solution.

Because the Culture Discourages Questions

Curiosity dwindles in situations where questioning the
status quo and questioning authority is discouraged.

Have a look at the text box below. Ask yourself how well your organization rates in these areas.

Reasons Why Companies and Leaders Discourage Curiosity and Questions at Work

While curiosity is often seen as a valuable trait, there are several reasons why companies and leaders might discourage it at work:

- Fear of Change:
  - Stability and Control: Companies may prioritize maintaining stability and control over their operations. Curiosity can lead to questioning established processes and systems, potentially disrupting the status quo.
  - Resistance to Innovation: Leaders might fear that encouraging curiosity will lead to a flood of new ideas and suggestions, which can be overwhelming and difficult to manage.

- Efficiency Concerns:
  - Productivity: There is a concern that curiosity-driven activities might divert employees' focus from their primary tasks, leading to decreased productivity.
  - Time Management: Exploring new ideas and experimenting can be time-consuming. Companies focused on short-term results may see this as a waste of valuable time and resources.

- Risk Aversion:
  - Unpredictability: Curiosity often involves exploring unknowns and taking risks. Companies with a risk-averse culture might discourage behaviours that could lead to unpredictable outcomes.

- Failure Tolerance: Organizations that have low tolerance for failure may not support curiosity-driven experimentation, fearing that it might lead to costly mistakes.
- Hierarchical Structures:
  - Top-Down Management: In companies with rigid hierarchical structures, curiosity can be seen as a challenge to authority. Leaders may discourage it to maintain their control and decision-making power.
  - Bureaucracy: Highly bureaucratic organizations might stifle curiosity through excessive rules and procedures, making it difficult for employees to explore new ideas.
- Resource Constraints:
  - Limited Resources: Companies with limited financial or human resources might discourage curiosity to focus on core activities and immediate goals.
  - Budgetary Restrictions: Curiosity-driven projects often require investment, and companies with tight budgets may be unwilling to allocate funds to uncertain outcomes.
- Cultural Factors:
  - Conformity: A corporate culture that values conformity over individuality can suppress curiosity. Employees may fear being perceived as troublemakers or non-team players.
  - Lack of Psychological Safety: If employees do not feel safe to express their ideas and ask questions, they will be less likely to exhibit curiosity.
- Performance Metrics:
  - Measurement Challenges: Curiosity and its outcomes are difficult to measure. Companies that rely heavily on quantifiable performance metrics might undervalue or overlook the benefits of curiosity.

(continued)

(*continued*)

- Focus on KPIs: An intense focus on key performance indicators (KPIs) and specific targets can discourage exploratory behaviour that does not directly contribute to these metrics.
- Lack of Understanding:
  - Misconceptions: Leaders may misunderstand curiosity as mere distraction or lack of discipline, rather than recognizing its potential to drive innovation and problem-solving.
  - Untrained Leadership: Leaders who are not trained to foster and manage curiosity may feel uncomfortable with it and therefore discourage it.

While these reasons highlight why curiosity and questions at work might be discouraged, it's important to note that fostering a culture of curiosity can lead to significant long-term benefits, including innovation, employee engagement, and adaptability. Balancing the need for stability and productivity with the encouragement of curiosity is a critical challenge for modern leaders.

Because We Lack the Skills Required to Ask the Needed Questions

This might sound trivial, but pay attention. Our upbringing plays an important role in our life. What we learn as kids shapes us as adults. We also learn to ask questions as children. The better we learn this skill from our parents, the better it will serve us later on. Curiosity is social. The more the parent engages with the questions of their children, the faster the child will learn how the world works. As a result the child will develop language faster, and do better at school. The child will also ask even more questions. Not only will the child learn the ways of the world, they will also learn how to formulate good questions.

Parental role modelling is crucial. What is not well understood is that the onus for asking questions not only lies with children, but also their parents. Research shows that it is not enough to respond to their questions, even more important is that parents also need to be initiating the questions with children. Research shows that parents who ask fewer questions are also more likely to issue prohibitions such as "stop" or "don't do that".[9]

One thing I did not fully understand when our four children were young was the role of technology. Though we allowed our young children to access the swiping wonders of the iPad as a way to explore the world, I realize now that the learning our children are exposed to when dealing with technology is far inferior to when they are in communication with adults. However well intentioned (and welcome after a day's hard work) it is that we give access to educational technology, it is not an equal substitute for a two-way question and answer session. If I could do things over, I would replace the iPad with a conversation. The iPad does not talk back. Curiosity is social and needs human interaction to grow.

The Power of Asking Deeper and Better Questions

Question consultant and author of *Change Your Questions, Change Your Life*, Marilee Adams PhD proposes a simple yet powerful tool to ask better and deeper questions.[10] She divides questions we have into two categories: judger questions and learner questions. Any questions, whether they are about the world, about others, or even about ourselves fall into one of these two categories. Such questions do not have to be articulated. They can be spoken, yet most often they are questions we ask ourselves internally, often even when we are not aware.

Marilee explained to me that judger questions are the default behaviour we normally have. Judger questions are intrinsically reactive, start from a fixed mindset, focus on blame, and are win–lose. Typical judger questions are, for instance: "What's wrong with me/them?", "Whose fault is it?", "Why bother?"

In her model, learner questions are the opposite of judger questions. These are questions which originate in a growth mindset and as such are uplifting. Such questions lead us to thoughtful choices, are proactive in nature, solution focused, and formulated in a win–win spirit. These are the hardest questions. Examples of learner questions are: "What can I learn from this situation?", "What assumptions am I making about other person or the situation?", "What are my choices?", "What options do I have?"

Through this process, once we become aware of our underlying question strategies, we have the choice to switch.

What Can I Do to Be a Better ...

Open questions are deeper questions. The tricky thing with open questions is that their answer can go in any direction. Asking, for example, "How much have you sold this month?" can be answered with a specific number of deals, value, and so on. That's a closed question. Asking on the other hand, "What do you need to sell more?" can lead to all kinds of responses, ranging from airing frustration to positive suggestions. Research has found that, globally, managers ask on average six questions per day.[11] First findings from large-scale research I am conducting points to the fact that more than 80% of questions leaders ask are closed questions.

Open questions are harder. As I alluded in Chapter 7, I have encouraged thousands of professionals to ask this simple question: "What can I do to be a better ...?" whereby one is invited to fill in the blank depending on the relationship. If one is a manager, one could ask: "What can I do to be a better boss?" If one is with a customer, one could ask: "How can I be a better supplier or business partner?" Or intimate partner, or child, or neighbour, or uncle, or sister ... you can use whatever relationship you have.

I first launched this exercise in Denmark at the Area 9 offices. The two co-founders of this learning tech company had invited me to do my book launch for their customers in their Copenhagen headquarters. I had been playing with this question, yet was afraid it was too simple to be shared with audiences, let alone executives; so with a bit of hesitation, I shared it the evening before with Khurram Jamil, one of the co-founders, at the small dinner he had invited me to the evening before the session. Copenhagen has wonderful restaurants.

When suggesting this question to him, Khurram was immediately fired up and started thinking of scenarios where this could be applicable at work. Then he moved to his family and immediately saw the deep power of this question. It's a deep question, and also a scary one. We don't know what the answer is going to be. Courage is needed. This conversation also gave me the courage and conviction that this question should be shared. Since then, I have encouraged thousands of professionals to use this question.

Can I Ask a Better Question?

"What would an outsider do?" is one of the questions London Business School professor Freek Vermeulen proposes.[12] In his work with global executives, Spenser Harrison, professor of organizational behaviour at INSEAD, uses this question as a stepping stone to new questions. Though the question is perfect on its own, Harrison invites people to not take this question at face value; to reflect on it, and see whether there could be an even better question.[13]

Think about this question for a second. How would you turn this question into a better one? Ask yourself: 'Can I ask a better question?" or raise this question next time you are in a meeting: "Can we ask a better question?"

Professor Harrison shares that you can also use this exercise in family situations. Think, for instance, about driving on a longer journey with your children. Eventually one of the children will ask: "Are we there yet?" You could reply: "Almost there" or "No we are not there yet, be quiet". Instead, another strategy is to play a game and say to the child: "That's a great question, could you ask a better question?" Chances are that the child will start looking around and ask questions about the landscape, the music, and so on and a conversation has just arisen. In the conversation, you can go back to your reply and invite the child to ask a better question at any point.

What Are We Not Seeing in the Data?

I have been consulting with a general manager of a US-based manufacturing company. Let's call him Paul. Paul is a champion for curiosity. He has invited me to speak to his leadership team, to his top 100 executives, and a number of his human resources managers have joined curiosity masterclasses at the Curiosity Institute. After internalizing the power of curiosity, Paul told me that he added a new question to his business review meetings: "What are we not seeing in the data?"

This simple question has triggered more openness in these meetings. Leaders know that they not only need to present their data, they need to go to the bottom of it and explore hypothesis, they need to go deep and question their numbers with a rigour they have not been used to. He has shared with me that this simple question has led to higher quality meetings, new hypotheses checking, better preparations, and has even led to new ideas about products and services, even upselling to customers.

As a leader, embracing new question strategies and promoting curiosity is not just an option; it is the key to unlocking untapped potential and achieving new heights of success. By cultivating a curiosity-driven culture, you empower your teams to innovate fearlessly, embrace diversity, and stay engaged on their journey of continuous improvement. So, if you are a leader, let curiosity be your guiding light, illuminating the path to a brighter, more prosperous future for your organization. We'll discuss the deep connection between curiosity and leadership in the next chapter. Are you ready to explore some more?

Questions for Reflection

- What is one significant insight you gained from this chapter about the power of asking better questions?
- How often do you find yourself refraining from asking questions in your professional life, and why do you think that is?
- Can you identify a recent situation where asking a better question at home or at work could have led to a different outcome? What question would you have asked?
- How can you incorporate the practice of asking open-ended questions into your daily routine to enhance your personal and professional growth?
- What is one specific action you can take this week to cultivate a more curious question mindset in yourself or your team?

Notes

1. Mittelstaedt, R.E. (2005). *Will Your Next Mistake Be Fatal?: Avoiding the Chain of Mistakes That Can Destroy Your Organization*. London: Pearson Education.
2. Glaveanu, V.P. (2020). *The Possible: A Sociocultural Theory*. Oxford: Oxford University Press.
3. Wass, S. (2017). Children ask parents 73 questions a day on average, study finds. *Study Finds*. https://studyfinds.org/children-parents-questions/ (accessed 31 October 2024).

4. Livio, M. (2017). *Why? What Makes Us Curious*. New York: Simon & Schuster.
5. Isaacs, N. (1930). *Intellectual Growth in Young Children*. California: Harcourt, Brace.
6. Harrison, S. and Cohen, J. (2018). *Curiosity Is Your Super Power* [TEDx Talk]. TEDxLosGatos. https://www.youtube.com/watch?v=xZJwMYeE9Ak (accessed 31 October 2024).
7. Marquardt, M.J. (2005). *Leading with Questions: How Leaders Find the Right Solutions by Knowing What to Ask*. Hoboken: Jossey-Bass.
8. Mittelstaedt, R.E. (2005). *Will Your Next Mistake Be Fatal? Avoiding the Chain of Mistakes That Can Destroy Your Organization*. London: Pearson Education.
9. Hart, B. and Risley, T.R. (1995). *Meaningful Differences in the Everyday Experience of Young American Children*. Maryland: Brookes Publishing.
10. Adams, M.G. and Marshall (2022). *Change Your Questions, Change Your Life*. Broadway: Berrett-Koehler Publishers.
11. Naughton, C. (2016). *Curiosity: How You Create Interest in Novelty and Change*. Berlin: Ullstein Buchverlage.
12. Vermeulen, F. (3 September 2015). *5 Strategy Questions Every Leader Should Make Time For*. Brighton: *Harvard Business Review*. https://hbr.org/2015/09/5-strategy-questions-every-leader-should-make-time-for (accessed 31 October 2024).
13. Harrison, S., & Cohen, J. (2017). *Pliable Guidance: A Multilevel Model of Curiosity, Feedback Seeking, and Feedback Giving in Creative Work*. https://journals.aom.org/doi/10.5465/amj.2015.0247

10

Leadership and Curiosity

"The leader of the past knew how to tell, the leader of the future must know how to ask."

Peter Drucker

Trigger Question: are underhand basketball free throws the more efficient way to score on a penalty?

Imagine you are a basketball coach. You pride yourself on having years of experience: you played at a fairly high level. Maybe not NBA level, yet you were pretty good nonetheless in your own league. Being older now, you still play the odd game. But your passion has shifted. You are a coach and a trainer now. And a good one. The girl's team you coach came out second last year in its competition league. It is the end of the season and with a bit of luck your team will become first. Or a good second, that's also fine.

Last week's game did not go as well as you had wished. The team won by three points, yet something happened. Something that bothers you. In the last minutes when things started getting nervous, one of your players took penalty shots. And did so underhand. You could not believe your eyes. What an inelegant way of taking a free shot, you thought. No wonder it is called the granny shot. She did score, however. Immediately afterwards and in the locker room, she became victim of quite some criticism, both on the court from the audience as well as from fellow players. You have not addressed the situation yet. Frankly you do not know how to deal with it. It is an ugly way to take a shot, yet denouncing the player openly does not feel right either. She scored, after all.

The modelling that a manager displays to the team is one of the biggest drivers of productivity, engagement, and the feeling of well-being. Managers who do this well lift the team. Those who don't stifle it. The key to effective task management and people leadership is curiosity. This is what we will explore together in this chapter.

Curious individuals need curious teams to thrive. The role of the leader in creating a conducive curiosity environment cannot be underestimated. Curiosity is a muscle, just like any muscle in the physical body. The more we use it, the bigger and stronger it gets. Stop using it, and it atrophies, becomes weak, and is prone to damage.

This is also true in teams. With the right permission, awareness, and intentionality, leaders build high performance teams. They know when to let curiosity take the lead and when not. They create an environment of receptivity and openness where new solutions and alliances can be born. Curiosity is gold to team building, talent retention, and overall well-being in the workplace.

Curious Organizations Are Run by Curious Leaders

Curious organizations are more successful than incurious ones, especially in times of change. Not only are they constantly looking for ways to improve their current operations, but they are also constantly scanning the business horizon for new opportunities. Curious organizations are led by curious leaders.

What would be your reaction as a coach to an employee pursuing an unconventional approach? You have a curious "employee" on your hands. Someone who is defying the status quo, someone who has the courage to stick out her neck, to try new things. Someone who has the courage to go beyond the conventional. Like the basketball player, someone who tries something new and takes a shot underhand.

You have two options, first: you can either do nothing and pretend you did not see anything; or second, you can take the person apart and advise her to stick to the "right" way of taking a shot. Maybe there is a third option: you can celebrate her action, back her up openly, and communicate to the team that people can take penalty shots how they like (as long as they score), even if it looks different or funny.

If you are a leader ready to train the curiosity muscle in the team, you will likely go for the last option. Doing nothing would leave everyone hanging. Siding with the majority would likely diminish any attempt by the team to take any other initiative in the foreseeable future. Your "underhand" shooting player might feel isolated.

Leaders who create curious workspaces invite more continuous improvement, adopt more innovation, create more engaged and productive teams. Curious leaders give permission to the team to challenge the status quo, help themselves and their team to become aware of underlying beliefs and are intentional in taking conducive action.

Not all leaders know how to create curious workplaces. According to a 2021 study by McKinsey, only 26% of leaders have the skills to create psychological safety for their teams.[1] Psychological safety is key for creating team curiosity. It's tricky for leaders. Often, they want the best of both worlds: all voices heard and failure acknowledged/learned from. But leaders also want harmony, comfort, and a sense of equilibrium. So many leaders end up creating a false "performative" version of psychological safety.

Those managers who are capable of it create psychologically safe environments that welcome dissenting voices and make minority opinions heard. They welcome curiosity into their teams.

Managers might consider giving their employees more independence: various studies show that a feeling of autonomy on the part of employees increases curiosity.

In a study conducted by Nicola Schutte and John Malouff, the effect of satisfying the basic psychological need for autonomy on curiosity was examined: 154 participants were randomly assigned to either a group which could choose a video to watch themselves, or another group which could not. All participants then rated their curiosity regarding the video's topic. Not surprisingly, the study found that the group which had the freedom to select the video to watch demonstrated higher curiosity levels than those without choice. This was also true for participants who had been found to have a low general autonomy need.[2]

These results underscore the importance of self-determination in fostering curiosity and have immediate application in the workspace. Let people self-select the projects they want to work on: even if there are only a limited number of options available, a project is more likely to stimulate someone's interest if they have selected it voluntarily.

Encourage workers to venture beyond their swimming lane. Invite employees to look beyond the narrow confines of their primary expertise. The increased interest in the new domain could then spill over into their own area, energizing their thinking and allowing them to spot new connections and lines of inquiry. When consulting for PepsiCo, I learned that they have established an internal project marketplace: employees are invited to join projects outside of their department for four to six hours per week. This helps them to learn a new part of the business, contribute to a novel project, acquire new understanding, and bring a new network of colleagues and new skills back to their day job.

One of the questions I get asked often is: how do I apply these insights in practice to create change in my own organization? A good starting point is to do the following.

- Embed curiosity and creativity in the job description and daily routine. Create time and space for people to be curious.
- Observe and communicate. Look for examples of what works and communicate best practices to the team.
- Shine a spotlight on employees who exemplify curious behaviour. To help the norm spread, you need to ensure everyone else sees it.
- Lavish the new behaviour with praise. People care deeply about receiving social rewards and copy the desired behaviour the manager praises—especially if they value the group.

Curiosity-driven leaders actively seek out new ideas, challenge existing paradigms, and embrace lifelong learning as a fundamental tenet of their leadership philosophy. By fostering a culture of curiosity within their teams and organizations, leaders encourage exploration, experimentation, and innovation, driving continuous improvement and adaptation in the face of change.

The Magic of the Underhand Free Throw

Could it be that shooting underhand is a much more efficient way to take a basketball penalty shot? Few professionals in the National Basketball Association (NBA) have tried this type of throw. Yet if they would, they would see their scoring percentages go through the roof. Rick Barry, renowned as one of the NBA's most exceptional players in history, employed a distinctive underhand technique for shooting free throws, achieving a remarkable 90% success rate throughout his illustrious 10-year career in the NBA. Remarkably, during his final two seasons, he attempted 322 free throws and missed merely 19, boasting an astonishing success rate of 94.1%.[3] In contrast, another basketball luminary, LeBron James, experienced a lower success rate, missing 132 shots in a single season, amounting to a 73.1% success rate. LeBron James threw his penalties overhand.[4]

You would think that a solid chunk of players would try underhand free throws. Not really. Why? Underhand shooting is perceived as being not cool. It is called the "sissy" or the "granny" shot. In a bold move during the 1962 season, basketball pro Wilt Chamberlain experimented with underhand free throws. Surprisingly, this adjustment led to a substantial increase in his scoring percentages, nearly doubling from 38% to an impressive 61%. Notably, this surpassed the average league scoring rate of 50.4% for that season by 10 percentage points. Despite his remarkable success with the underhand technique, Chamberlain opted to revert to shooting overhand. In his autobiography, he elaborated on the reasoning behind this decision: "I felt silly, like a sissy, shooting underhand. I just couldn't do it."[5] Brave acts of non-conformity are tragically rare. Leaders who actively encourage the team to be non-conformist are also rare.

Curious leaders are good at operationalizing the present as well as securing the future. They create psychological safety for the team to thrive. Curious leaders represent a high level of cognitive, empathic, and self-reflective curiosity. They are curious about the world around them, the people they work with, and their own internal conscious and unconscious drivers. They go out of their way to engage with their team, also in times of crisis. They stretch their teams to excel in the present and embrace the future. In communicating with others, curious leaders give undivided attention and are mindful in the moment.

Though many leaders see themselves as role models of curiosity and openly say they value inquisitive minds, in fact, many prefer conformity and stifle curiosity within their teams. However, with the right permission, awareness, and intentionality, leaders can become better at their own curiosity and at the same time create the right curious environment for their teams.

The Say/Do Ratio of Curiosity at Work

Since the beginning of the century and more specifically in the post COVID-19 era, the world of business has been changing dramatically. In times of radical change, leaders realize that "milking" past successes will not take them very far. As a result, good leaders embrace openness towards an unknown future. Those leaders that balance both exploitation and exploration will keep their organizations competitive. *Saying* this is easy, *doing* this is harder. Intentional curiosity is of paramount importance in times of change.

The Importance of Workplace Curiosity

A 2018 study by Francesca Gino at the Harvard Business School provides three insights into the importance and implications of workplace curiosity.[6]

First, curiosity is more important for business success than previously thought. In times of industrial stability, curiosity is limited to continuous improvement as products and services remain relevant for many years. Eastman-Kodak was able to sell its products and services for 100 years given the world of analogue photography did not change much. Once digital photography replaced analogue photography, Eastman-Kodak had lost its exploration mindset. In times of instability, companies find their environments change constantly and need to be open to respond to changes if they want to remain competitive.

Second, companies can change the way they approach curiosity. By making small changes to the design of their organization and the ways they manage employees, leaders can encourage curiosity and improve their companies. When Satya Nadella became CEO at Microsoft in February 2014, one of the first things he did was to change the ingrained culture of "know-it-all" behaviour his predecessor left behind. He replaced it with a culture where "learn-it-all" was the norm,

(continued)

(*continued*)

where leaders could admit they did not have all the answers and, as a result, invite the entire team to collectively come up with the solution. You don't have to be a CEO to change the culture. Through active role modelling and intentional action, leaders at all levels can create a curiosity conducive culture in their own teams.

The third thing Ms Gino found was that most leaders actually stifle curiosity rather than encourage it. Though most leaders say they value inquisitive minds, in fact most crush curiosity through the conformist cultures they create and through the belief that curiosity jeopardizes efficiency and increases risk. On the one hand, executives realize the underlying importance of curiosity in helping to implement their firm's strategy agenda when it comes to product and services innovation, outwitting competition, winning deals, taking calculated risks in the pursuit of novel and creative outcomes, etc. On the other hand, these same executives reject curiosity as something which goes against the grain of operational efficiency of the organization.

Hold on. An overwhelming percentage of leaders self-declare that they are excellent at curiosity and often consider themselves superior in curiosity. I have so far only met two brave senior executive souls who were humble enough to downplay their curiosity, one board member and a corporate shared services executive. Maybe all the others are deluding themselves. Maybe they have a narrow view of curiosity. Or they really are the real deal. When I ask the same leaders whether curiosity is a good thing for an organization, 90% respond in the affirmative.

When I inquire then whether they invite curiosity in their teams and in their daily operations, only 52% admit to doing so.

Their say/do ratio is off. What they are saying is that in theory curiosity is a good thing. What they are also saying is that they prefer others to pick it up. It is more important to judge leaders by what they do, not what they say.

In a cross-industry curiosity study funded by the German healthcare and life-sciences giant, Merck, several curiosity barriers associated with leaders were found. The first barrier they found was that autocratic, top-down leadership behaviour stifles curiosity as curious subordinates are not provided with the opportunity to question or challenge decisions, nor are they invited to explore and share novel options. Another barrier was that the prevalence of risk-averse behaviour makes leaders opt for proven and safe ideas, thus restricting creative thinking time. Also, a preference for conformity on the side of the manager and fear of standing out from others among managerial peers.[7]

In many organizational cultures, the downside of being curious about an alternative version of the future and taking risks is often greater than its upside. Suggesting and implementing a new idea is a lonely business when things go south, and potential failures can limit career mobility and decrease year-end bonus potential. It is often easier to stay the collective course rather than be the lonely warrior for change, even when change is needed.

They are not entirely wrong about this: curiosity by its very nature slows us—and things—down. If you are in the middle of a customer deadline, you don't want to challenge the status quo.

This does not mean that curiosity is hard to do at all stages of work. When starting a project, it is common sense to take time out and ask some basic questions, clarify assumptions, and agree collectively on a way forward. Common sense, however, is not always common practice. Many projects move into implementation before the ground rules have been agreed upon.

Slowing down at the beginning of projects and asking questions like: "What are we setting out to do?", "What are our options?", "What can we learn from past projects to better implement this project?", "Are we all on board?" guarantees less friction, less scope creep, and more in-time and in-budget delivery. It takes a strong leader to guide the team to slow down in the initial phases of a project. Once the leader has created the time, space, and psychological safety in the first project phase, she can move the team into the implementation phase during which the focus is on delivering what the team agreed upon. Curiosity at the implementation stage moves to a secondary role. In the implementation phase, the team remains open to continuous improvement yet leaves the agreed big strokes of the project untouched.

Curiosity also has enormous value at the end of a project. Long term value. Project post-mortems or after-action reviews solidify organizational learning. At the end of the project, leaders guide the team to explore the following questions. "What was expected to happen?", "What actually occurred?", "What went well and why?", "What can be improved and how?" Curiosity helps to ensure success at the beginning of a project and captures learning at the end of a project. It is not whether you should challenge the status quo, but when you should do it.

Allowing curiosity in the beginning and at the end of projects improves the quality of output as well as that of future projects, yet it does not come without a cost. Groups who do this well might experience twice as much controversy in battling alternative viewpoints as compared to homogenous groups.[8] Positivity, cohesion, and short-term decision-making can take a temporary hit. It requires a mature, humble, and confident leader to guide the team through this process. When done well, however, curiosity supercharges the team into taking better and deeper decisions, making deeper intrapersonal connections, and giving stronger ownership on the part of each of the team members.

How to do this? How can leaders encourage teams to feel comfortable to adopt a non-conformist mindset in the beginning and at the end of projects? By explicitly welcoming all team members to do so. Don't merely offer them a welcome mat. Actively affirm the significance of curiosity within the group. Reinforce the notion that it requires courage to voice one's thoughts. Emphasize how curiosity shields the team from making superficial and poorly thought-out decisions. Highlight the necessity for novel ideas and distinctive solutions, inviting every member to contribute their unique skills. Make sure every team member gets heard, including the quieter ones. Recognize diversity of thought as a vital component of the decision-making process.

Leaders as Curiosity Role Models

We have discussed that the role of the leader is crucial in helping the team to rise above itself. Leaders are often not sufficiently aware of the impact their actions have on their team's behaviour. The extent of their intellectual curiosity has a huge impact on the curiosity of their team members. When I was chief learning officer at the global IT services company Cognizant, I had the chance to study the intellectual impact of the leader on the team. To study this, we looked at knowledge consumption data within the company, namely at all possible instructional information like (e) classes, books, webinars, conferences. Using this data, we calculated the time each manager invested in their growth. Then we looked at similar data for their team members.

In reviewing the substantial data group of 30,000 leaders, we found a linear correlation between the leader's learning profile and that of the team. If the manager consumes a lot of information, so does the team. At first this does not strike one as remarkable, but rather intuitive. When digging deeper, however, we found that it is not the learning hours that are important, but the subtle message of desired behaviour that the leader projects to the team and the simple actions the leader conveys, such as sharing articles, new insights, interesting data points. Once the team picks up that there is an underlying expectation that intellectual curiosity is seen as positive by the leader, they follow suit.

Another finding from the data was worrying: when the leader does not invest time in learning, the team falls flat in their consumption of learning too. When conducting focus groups, we found that managers are often not aware of the impact their own behaviour has on the team. Simply highlighting the impact of their actions on the team is often enough for them to reflect, give permission, become aware, and take action. Leaders can cultivate a culture of curiosity by leading by example.

Being a role model means being effective at listening, i.e. listening to understand instead of listening to respond. And asking a lot of questions, open questions. And using the right type of language.

That the language leaders use affects team members has been researched by Spencer Harrison, professor of organizational behaviour at INSEAD. Professor Harrison studied the daily logs of teams on the planet Mars. More specifically, he looked at teams of people who simulate being on Mars for the sole purpose of studying life and group relations in harsh and remote human settlements planned for in the future on Mars. In desert-based Mars simulators, scientists and volunteers are invited to act like they live on Mars. At the end of each day, each member is invited to update their experiences in a logbook. When the logbooks of leaders are compared to those of the team members, something curious happens.

Professor Harrison used linguistic text analysis of the logbooks of the team leads. What he found was that the use of question marks (an indicator of asking questions), as well as exclamation points (a reflection of surprise) has a direct effect on the logbooks of the team members. Simply put, the more questions and surprises the team lead wrote, the more curious language (words like: novel, invent, discover, new, curious ...) was found in the team members' logbooks the day after. He found a standard deviation in question marks and/or exclamation points the day before also led to a change in standard deviation of the use of curious words of the team members the day after.[9] There is an important message here for leaders: the written or spoken language leaders use in emails and interactions has a direct effect on how people around them behave.

Once managers become aware of their actions, permission and intentional behaviour becomes easier. I recently encouraged a leader to take a curious action in a tense interpersonal manager–team member situation: to lean in to being wrong instead of clinging to his desire to be right. I invited the leader to be fully present, listen deeply, ask open questions, and repeat the answers in his own words to let the other person know that he heard her. In short: slow down, focus on the other person, be curious without judgement, and minimize distractions. The result he shared was remarkable: "My colleague visibly relaxed before my eyes, shifting from a defensive stance to one of receptiveness. Rather than rigidly adhering to my own ideas, I found myself offering a fresh perspective in the moment. By remaining open and adaptable, I was able to leverage the information presented and pivot towards a more effective strategy. The result? Our subsequent actions were met with success as we translated our ideas into tangible outcomes."

One study revealed that individuals who report their leader consistently responding constructively to challenges are approximately 12 times more inclined to recommend their employer as a great place to work.[10] This is the power of curiosity.

Psychological Safety and Minority Viewpoints

Psychological safety is key to creating high performing and high trust teams. Plenty has been written about this phenomenon since Amy Edmondson coined the phrase in the 1990s to describe work environments where candour is expected and where employees can speak up without fear of retribution.[11] Since then, organizations have undertaken a "safe place" revolution in the hope of boosting motivation, learning, performance, and innovation. And yet, research has shown psychological safety does not correlate with performance. For some teams it works, for other it does not. In the words of Todd Kashdan: "Psychological safety reliably translates into superior performance only when sufficient minority view-points exist, and we permit and embrace them when present."[12] Allowing our basketball player to throw underhand would thus be the right thing to do.

There is a common belief that the positional power of the leader comes with the burden of superior knowledge. Once in power, the leader is supposed to be (and look) strong, articulate all questions before the team does, and have all the answers. His expert status should not be challenged. Inviting non-conformist ideas and thinking might challenge the voice of the leader and overall distract the team from delivering their required output. An important reason for this disconnect, or rather illusion, is that leaders fear to lose their control over and focus of the team.

When assuming a leadership role, there's often immense pressure to demonstrate competence and possess all the answers. Regrettably, this pressure erects a barrier to curiosity. Having all the answers not only fails to cultivate engagement, motivation, and productivity, but also stifles innovation.

Encouraging input from the entire team necessitates leaders' willingness to embrace the possibility of being mistaken or to entertain alternative perspectives. This can be challenging for many leaders, as they often attribute their higher compensation to their perceived expertise and problem-solving abilities. In the eyes of many leaders, not knowing is a sign of weakness.

Unbeknownst to many managers, however, respect increases every time the manager says "I do not know". By posing open questions, projecting humility, and actively seeking knowledge, the leader prioritizes listening and understanding over immediate responses and being correct. Curiosity is about letting go of being right. It entails entering every discussion, strategy session, or challenging conversation with an active spirit of inquiry and receptivity.

When executed effectively, this approach yields palpable results and creates a noticeable shift towards increased openness and consensus during interactions. Why does this occur? Typically, in meetings, our attention is narrowly focused on our own agenda and objectives. We firmly believe in the correctness of our viewpoints, which leads us to tune out opposing perspectives. This inclination is a fundamental aspect of human nature. We selectively attend to information that validates our beliefs, inadvertently overlooking crucial insights that could either challenge our assumptions or fortify our positions.

Many of us have encountered situations where we're interrupted mid-sentence, with the listener interjecting with opinions or responses that disregard our previous remarks entirely. Such experiences can be exasperating, highlighting the absence of curiosity in the interaction. This phenomenon is relatable—it's something I've encountered, and you likely have too. It's not typically driven by malicious intent but rather by ingrained human tendencies, particularly pronounced in environments characterized by high pressure, competition, and distraction. Curious leaders avoid this because they are intentional about listening.

Curious leaders also practise reverse feedback as we discussed in Chapter 1. Reverse feedback, i.e. asking: "How am I doing as your boss?" is a powerful way for leaders to unleash the power of curiosity in their team. By setting an example of being vulnerable, humble, and open to feedback, leaders set the stage for more openness. Though intuitively leaders recognize reverse feedback as common sense, it does not seem to be a common practice. According to my research at the Global Curiosity Institute, only 26% of front line leaders are asking how they are doing of their team (versus 46% of middle managers and 6% senior leaders). On what side of the equation are you or do you want to be?

What about shifting gears? There is lots of talk about Artificial Intelligence at present. Is AI a curiosity friend or foe? We know that our brains and memory are not operating under the same paradigm of a hard disk as early thinkers wanted to believe. Let's explore how AI corresponds with curiosity in the next chapter.

Questions for Reflection

- How do you manage the tension between maintaining operational efficiency and fostering a culture of curiosity and exploration?
- Consider the "underhand free throw" metaphor. What are some unconventional practices in your industry that could lead to significant improvements if adopted them?
- How do you currently balance directive leadership with encouraging curiosity and inquiry within your team?
- How do you currently handle feedback from your team? What steps can you take to encourage more open and honest communication?
- Reflect on a time when a team member proposed an unconventional idea. How did you respond, and what was the outcome?

Notes

1. McKinsey & Company (2021). Just 26 percent of leaders create psychological safety for their teams. https://www.mckinsey.com/featured-insights/sustainable-inclusive-growth/chart-of-the-day/just-26-percent-of-leaders-create-psychological-safety-for-their-teams (accessed 31 October 2024).
2. Schutte, N.S. and Malouff, J.M. (2019). *Increasing Curiosity Through Autonomy of Choice*. Armidale: University of New England. doi:10.1007/s11031-019-09758-w, https://hdl.handle.net/1959.11/26466 (accessed 31 October 2024).

3. Donahue, B. The life and career of Rick Barry. https://www.basketballhistory.org/rick-barry/ (accessed 25 September 2024).

4. Lineups.com. LeBron James NBA Player Stats. https://www.lineups.com/nba/player-stats/lebron-james (accessed 25 September 2024).

5. Chamberlain, W. and Shaw, D. (1973). *Wilt: Just Like Any Other 7-Foot Black Millionaire Who Lives Next Door*. York: Macmillan.

6. Gino, F. (2018). The business case for curiosity. *Harvard Business Review* 96 (5): 48–57. https://hbr.org/2018/09/the-business-case-for-curiosity (accessed 31 October 2024).

7. Merck KGaA. (2020). *State of Curiosity Report*. https://www.merckgroup.com/en/news/2020-state-of-curiosity-report-28-01-2021.html (accessed 31 October 2024).

8. Kashdan, T.B. (2022). *The Art of Insubordination: How to Dissent and Defy Effectively*. California: Avery.

9. Spencer, H. (2021). *Your Super Power Curiosity. The Curious Advantage Podcast, Produced by Paul Ashcroft, Simon Brown and Garrick Jones*. https://podcasts.apple.com/cz/podcast/your-superpower-curiosity-the-curious-advantage-podcast/id1509018267?i=1000519222390 (accessed 31 October 2024).

10. Schaufeli, W.B. (2021). The impact of engaging leadership on employee engagement and team effectiveness: A longitudinal, multi-level study on the mediating role of personal- and team resources. *PLoS ONE* 17 (6): e0269433. https://doi.org/10.1371/journal.pone.0269433 (accessed 31 October 2024).

11. Edmondson, A.C. (2019). *The Fearless Organization: Creating Psychological Safety in the Workplace for Learning, Innovation, and Growth*. New Jersey: Wiley.

12. Kashdan, T.B. (2022). *The Art of Insubordination: How to Dissent and Defy Effectively*. California: Avery.

11

Alchemy and AI

"Artificial intelligence will be either the best, or
worst thing, ever to happen to humanity."
Stephen Hawking, Theoretical Physicist

**Trigger Question: how curious are you about new
technology such as Artificial Intelligence (AI); does
it excite you or worry you?**

L et's play a game. It is actually a game you can play
next time you have friends over to your place.
We'll call it "the Imitation Game". The rules of the
game are simple: select in your group one man and
one woman and ask both to go into a separate room
so they are out of sight. Ask them to flip a coin to
establish who will be A and who will be B from that
point on. Everyone else at the party will communicate with them by means of written questions slipped
under the door addressed to either A or B. Both will
write answers on the slips and send them back. With
written communication, both the man and the woman's job is to convince your other guests that they are ...
the woman. By asking clever questions, the guests
need to determine whether it's really A or it is B that
is the woman. Do you think you could come up with
questions that would tell you who is who?

What if one of the two is a machine and instead
of written notes, you have a keyboard. Would you
be able to establish with your questions who is who?
In other words, would the computer be able to give
responses that are indistinguishable from those of a

thinking person? And if yes, can a machine be trained to think like people? In short: can computers become as smart as people? Can they become as curious as you and me? We know from our experience with Google that they can answer questions, yet can they ask good and curious questions too? This is what we will discuss in this chapter.

Robots Augmenting Humans

One of our greatest assets is our ability to think. Logical thinking and mathematical calculation in particular are essential and powerful human abilities. Both require a great deal of tedious brain power and effort. Throughout history humans have tried to make it easier on themselves. We've tried to develop ways that let us get the same results with less effort. The history of technology is a history of machines invented for two purposes: on the one hand to avoid the toil and trouble of physical labour and on the other hand to give us more power. How the tools look matters little: they can be big heavy mechanical tools like a tractor, an industrial robot, a smartphone, an algorithm telling us we need to exercise, or ChatGPT helping us with writing a school paper or writing a customer proposal or upgrading our resume.

People have long been fascinated with machines that act like people. What do we see in robots or in technology? What makes them so fascinating? The word "robot" is in fact a recent invention. It first appeared in a play in Prague in 1921. Rossems' Universal Robots by the playwright Karel Capek. Robot was an adaptation of a Czech word for "tedious labour".

Although robot is a recent term, the idea of an artificial human is a very old one. Homer's *Iliad*, written in about 800 BC, has several references to robots. Hephaistos, the Greek blacksmith god who created Achilles' armour, has robot-like assistants— "golden maid-servants hastening to help their master". They seemed to have looked like real girls and also possessed intelligence and were trained to help the immortal god. Hephaistos also had other robots made. According to Homer, he had created a number of three legged tables, each fitted with golden wheels so they could run by themselves to a meeting of the gods and amaze them by running home again.

Humanoid robots are made to look like people, like the God's golden maid-servants. By contrast, Hephaistos' self-propelled tables were autonomous non-humanoid robots. These are not the only robots in ancient myth. In Minoan Crete, there was said to be a bronze giant named Telos who patrolled the edges of the island to repel any enemies. These myths describe robots in terms of supporting their master Hephaestus and the Olympian gods and also assign to them the roles of powerful protectors of humans against enemies in the story of Telos. What both had in common was they were mechanical and created by man.

Sometimes the creators are less mechanically inclined, creating robots from inanimate matter. There is, for example, the myth of Pygmalion which was first described in Ovid's metamorphoses, completed in Rome in 8 AD. The story goes that artist Pygmalion is a misogynist. Nonetheless, he creates a sculpture in the shape of a woman and falls in love with that sculpture. Venus, the goddess of love, conveniently steps in and makes the statue real. They both run off and bear a child. This is the kind of myth that never dies. Pygmalion represents a romantic side of our ancient fascination with robots.

Recurring themes surrounding artificially created things and beings are creation, protection, support, power, even sexual attraction and love.

Nowadays, we accept technology in most parts of our lives. Technology promises to make our lives easier and more powerful. Some of us are more comfortable with adopting technology than others. Age matters. Alan Kay, Chief Technology Officer of the Xerox Paolo Alto Research Centre rightfully said[1]:

"Technology is anything that was invented after you were born, everything else is just stuff."

In my own history, computers came "later" in life. I got my first computer when I was 20 years old, the year I graduated from university. I needed to write my Master's thesis and my father and I thought it was a good idea to buy one of these machines. This makes me a digital immigrant, meaning that I have an "accent" when speaking about things digital. Even when I think I am quite good at it, my kids are infinitely better. For them, computers are part of the furniture, so "stuff".

Let's look at the global adoption of technology. Good marketing, good timing, and the promise of greater efficiency and productivity is accelerating the speed of digital development. How long did it take for mobile phones to reach sales of 100 million? 16 years. For the Internet to reach 100 million users: 7 years. For Facebook to reach the same metric: 4.5 years.

And how long did it take for ChatGPT to reach 100 million subscribers? Two months. That is not a typo.

The Dark Side of Technology

As mentioned, the story of robots and by extension artificial intelligence is one of creation, power, protection, support, even love. In the twentieth century, a new set of new connotations was added to this list, namely the dark side of technology. Robots are associated more and more with "things gone wrong". Murderous robots have been clearly established as a theme in Hollywood and beyond. Think of Arnold

Schwarzenegger in the first "Terminator" being sent from the future to kill humanity, or the artificial intelligence Hal in 2001 "A Space Odyssey" who tries to kill the entire astronaut crew aboard the spaceship.

Alongside the killer robot, another theme has been growing; namely, the theme of nascent and sympathetic robot consciousness. Arnold Schwarzenegger shifts his sympathies to the human side in the later "Terminator" sequels. For fans of "Star Wars", R2D2 and C3PO are sympathetically comic throughout the series.

Traditional versus Generative AI

Let's dive a bit deeper into the world of computers and artificial intelligence and see how curiosity fits. Let's start by asking: is the computer a curiosity machine and is the Internet making us smarter and more curious?

Remember the game we played at the beginning of this chapter? It was invented by the person who was as historically important for contemporary artificial intelligence as Einstein was for contemporary physics. His name was Alan M. Turing: a British mathematician and logician during World War II. Turing was instrumental in cracking the Enigma code: the code the Nazi's used for transmitting their strategic secrets. In 1950, Turing published an article in which he proposed a test for machine intelligence which has come to be known as the Turing test.

Turing offered a prediction that machines would be able to take the Turing test 50 years later, in the year 2000, after which he thought machine answers would be unrecognizable from human ones. He also invented the first generation of machine learning.

The concept of machine learning is simple. Until recently, machine learning was the main form of artificial intelligence we've been used to. Computers were fed with all kinds of information; questions and simple answers to these very questions. This type of artificial intelligence was used, among other things, to support online bots on websites, it supported radiologists in pre-scanning x-rays, and offered a first set of recommendations to the doctors.

Turing's invention also led to the invention of the IBM computer program Deep Blue. On 10 February 1996, Deep Blue became the first chess computer to beat a reigning World Champion, Garry Kasparov, in a game under tournament conditions. This happened in the first Kasparov vs Deep Blue match, the first big "Man vs Machine" match. Despite his loss in the first game Kasparov still won the match 4–2; but one year later, on 11 May 1997, he lost a rematch against Deep Blue. Deep Blue, with its enormous processing power of 100–200 million potential chess moves per second, also had access to a database of nearly one million grandmaster games for reference.

Traditional AI was deterministic and predictable. It could work with the set of information it was fed, and—as the Deep Blue example shows—was very good at it. Deep Blue could not, however, go beyond chess. In psychological terms, it can be compared to an idiot savant, a person who has an exceptional aptitude in one area, yet lacks skills in virtually all other areas. With all its processing speed, Deep Blue could not tell you how to go about simply boiling an egg. We would have to wait for generative AI to help us with our breakfast.

The world of computing has not been standing still since 1997. We know that computers can defeat humans at chess, we even expect it. However, when Google's AlphaZero program defeated the Stockfish 8 program in chess, we looked again, not knowing whether we were observing a divine miracle or should be scared.

Stockfish 8 was the world's most powerful computer chess program until 2016. It was able to compute 70 million chess positions per second and—not unlike Deep Blue—could reference a database filled with decades of chess moves and games in a split second. In contrast, AlphaZero only had the processing power to perform 80,000 computations per second and it did not have a huge chess moves database to rely on. Even more remarkable, its human creators never taught it any chess strategies, not even standard openings. AlphaZero learned chess by playing against itself. Guess how long AlphaZero needed to be ready to defeat the powerful Stockfish 8 program? Four hours. Yes, four hours ... AlphaZero went from utter ignorance to absolute mastery in four hours, without the help of a human intervention.[2] In the 100 games both computer programs played, AlphaZero won 28, and tied 72. It did not lose once.

Computer programming and processing power is advancing so fast that we are facing a paradigm shift comparable to the invention of the printing press by Johannes Gutenberg in 1439.

In 2016, the physicist Stephen Hawking predicted that the creation of artificial intelligence would be "either the best, or worst thing, ever to happen to humanity". And that "success in creating AI could be the biggest event in the history of our civilization".[3] Normally I am wary of people outside their field of expertise making authoritative predictions, like actors or social media influencers making claims on the usefulness of COVID-19 vaccination. In the case of Stephen Hawking, I make an exception, and with good reason. Having a brother-in-law astrophysicist in the family, I understand how much computing power and advanced software is part of the tool-kit of physicists.

Generative AI is changing the way we recruit, learn, and work in the digital workplace. It might even change the way we interface with our doctors and therapists. Yogesh Kumar, a data products leader active in e-commerce and data privacy areas and possessing of a highly curious mind when it comes to AI, told me that a simple audio recording of five minutes of speaking is enough for AI to understand us and have a meaningful therapeutic discussion about some of our mental challenges, like burnout or stress. This could be scary on the one hand, the idea that technology is potentially taking over jobs in areas we deem reserved solely for humans. However, if you are living in a small town in rural India where there are no specialists to help you, a digital therapist might be a welcome choice given there are no real therapists around. In addition, you don't need to wait for days to fit into the busy schedule of the digital therapist. On the contrary, it/he/she will be available whenever you need it/him/her, even on a Sunday evening if you want.

When checking clinical and counselling psychologists on the site "willrobotstakemyjob.com" the site only tells me that 7% of these jobs are in danger of being automated. Other jobs are more in the line of fire. According to this site, paralegals and legal assistants have an 89% likelihood of being replaced. This site has been around for a couple of years and was created during the first wave of AI. I am not sure whether its makers have updated the site now that we are in the second wave.

"While traditional AI was linked to automation and blue collar jobs were more at risk," Yogesh Kumar said to me, "generative AI will challenge job security for white collar employees."

Kumar predicts that there will be even a potential downward salary spiral for white collar employees, especially those white collar employees who have been able to perform only at average levels up to the present and those who have not kept their knowledge and skill-sets up to date.

In a very real sense, although generative AI is able to create mesmerizing output, it is heavily reliant on what it can scrape together from the Internet. At this moment, it is not capable of creating novel thoughts or creating new innovations. Generative AI is wonderful at recreating an advert for your company provided it has something lying around on the worldwide web to work from, but don't ask it to create something radically new. In the words of Ray Nayler, visiting scholar at the George Washington University's Institute of International Science and Technology Policy: "Simply put: AI thrives when our need for originality is low and our demand for mediocrity is high."[4]

I experienced the power of the digital world recently when helping my son create a website for his new restaurant. The platform I used gave me more than just the right templates to create a professional site. It augmented my own powers dramatically—I was able to create a new site without help from a web designer. To create his logo, I got help from ChatGPT. I described in the ChatGPT prompt that my son was creating a high quality, modern yet traditional Japanese noodle restaurant and asked it to suggest about 10 designs for a logo. Within milliseconds, I had 10 good enough logos my son could choose from. "Good enough" was good enough for him to get started.

Yet good enough also has a dark side. Is "good enough" also our reaction to food and to other things in life? What is our reaction to mediocrity as consumers? I did not realize what I was missing until I tasted my own home-grown tomatoes. It was as if a new taste revealed itself, one that I had been deprived of my entire life. Without realizing it, my demand for quality tomatoes had been low.

Ray Nayler picks up on this question in a November 2023 *Time Magazine* article with the juicy title "AI and the Rise of Mediocrity": "But a topic less explored," he writes, "is that mechanization also demands a replaceable consumer: a target to be manipulated into purchasing low-quality products they do not need—and that they did not actually want. In the end, mechanization's real innovation is in manipulating consumer demand: creating a complacent buyer with reduced expectations of quality. Once you've done that, you can sell them a 'good enough' widget. You have to create a person willing to spend a pain-inducing amount of money on upgrading to an only marginally better phone."

Are We Getting Collectively Smarter With AI?

If Alan Turing were to come back from the 1950s to the present and observe how most people use technology nowadays, my guess is that he would write something like this in his diary: "My wildest dreams about computing power and artificial intelligence have come true. People now possess a pocket-size device on which they can access the entirety of information known to man. Strangely however, they use it to look at pictures of cats and get into arguments with strangers."

We have seen earlier in this chapter that we are a lazy species. The moment we are given a new tool, we run with it. I would hate to go back to the time without GPS. However, this begs the question whether tools like the Internet are actually good for us. It is a fair question to ask whether the Internet is making us smarter or dumber. The answer is a qualified: yes—both!

On the one hand, technology gives us almost anything we want to learn. Want to learn how people lived in Pompeii AD 57? How the Mars Rover— not incidentally named "curiosity"—is fuelled? How Facebook tricks you into believing we have free will? Or how to get a degree in beekeeping? It's all available online. You have to put in the time and effort, yet if you are really motivated, it is all readily available and mostly even for free. The Internet and all its applications can definitely make you smarter.

On the other hand, the entertainment value of the Internet overshadows its educational value. According to Statista, in 2024 we spend on average 6 hours and 30 minutes on the Internet daily, of which 2 hours and 13 minutes is spent on social media.[5] We discussed in this book that when looking at how humanity consumes the Internet, we see that the vast majority of our time is spent in non-learning activities. A normal

Facebook user spends around 7 hours, 45 minutes and 49 seconds per month on Facebook.[6] In reviewing a sample of 20,000 people in China, researchers found that 36.7% of the population are Internet addicts, of which 2.8 % have a severe Internet addiction. For a country like China, this amounts to 39.5 million people having severe Internet addiction. To put this in perspective, 39.5 million is roughly 50% of the total German population.[7]

The jury is still out on whether we are becoming smarter; yet only a very few people seem to be escaping the Internet's laziness grip.

With a global proliferation of access to research because of the Internet, we could easily imagine that academic research has become richer and that academics are reaping its rewards. Not quite. James Evans, a sociologist at the University of Chicago, reviewed a database of thirty-four million academic papers published between 1945 and 2005. He analyzed the citations added at the back of the research papers to see whether patterns of research had changed when comparing print to online access. He found that as journals went online, scholars actually cited fewer articles than they had before.[8]

There are a number of hypotheses on why this is happening. First, search algorithms present the most popular links rather than the most useful ones. Researchers are humans too and cognitive laziness makes them prefer the first page of search results over subsequent pages. Another hypothesis according to Evans is that in the old days, researchers would routinely flip through research magazines such as *Science* or *Nature* and at times stumble upon new insights from related or even unrelated fields. These serendipitous intellectual encounters with articles are happening much less due to the ease and efficiency of hyperlink searches.

Students in general may also experience some of the shortcomings of AI. In a study of 285 Pakistani and Chinese university students, the data analysis findings show that AI causes significant loss of human decision-making and makes humans lazy. I have long been of the opinion that the more we delegate our brain capacity to tools like Google or ChatGPT, the more we restrict internal growth. Learning takes time and energy and does not take shortcuts. I fully agree with the authors of the study that governments should study AI in detail and adopt preventive measures before implementing AI technology in education.[9]

Yogesh Kumar highlighted an intrinsic danger of generative AI tools like ChatGPT. "If you have experienced a tool like ChatGPT," Kumar shared, "you have been exposed to a challenge: one of confidence. ChatGPT presents its knowledge as truth and unless you have previous knowledge about the subject you are inquiring about, it is hard for you to assess whether this confidence and impeccable grammar is also true."

What Strategies Can Mortals Adopt?

We might not automatically become smarter without effort, yet a hybrid approach seems to be working in the professional sphere. Those professionals who are using AI as part of their work create more output and are more efficient than peers who don't. Researchers at Harvard Business School studied the impact of AI on knowledge worker productivity and quality. They examined how ChatGPT-4 affected the work of 758 Boston consulting group consultants. The results showed that consultants using ChatGPT-4 outperformed their counterparts. They finished 12.2% more tasks on average, completed tasks 25.1% more quickly, and produced results of 40% higher quality compared to those without AI support.[10]

In the world of new technology, it pays to be curious, to lean into our anxiety, to slow down and study the merits (and limitations) of the new technology.

I hope I piqued your curiosity when it comes to technology. Are you ready to be intrigued by another dimension where curiosity makes or breaks the outcome? Curious professionals need curious organizations. Curious organizations are organizations who value curiosity in the fabric of their corporate culture. We will be exploring the power of curiosity and corporate culture in the following chapter.

Questions for Reflection

- What do you think of Stephen Hawking's view on AI as potentially the best or worst thing for humanity? Do you agree or disagree, and why?
- Reflect on a time when technology significantly reduced your cognitive load or increased your efficiency. How did this impact your work or personal life?
- Consider the historical fascination with machines mimicking human behaviour. What do you think this says about human nature and our desire for technological advancement?
- How has the rapid adoption of digital technologies, like ChatGPT, changed your daily life or professional practice? Provide specific examples.
- How can professionals develop a proactive and curious mindset to harness the full potential of AI in their work? What steps can you take to embrace continuous learning and practical application of AI?

Notes

1. Robson, D. (2024). Why we have co-evolved with technology. https://www.bbc.com/future/article/20240404-why-we-have-co-evolved-with-technology-tom-chatfield-wise-animals (accessed 6 April 2024).

2. Harari, Y.N. (2018). *21 Lessons for the 21st Century*. New York: Spiegel & Grau.

3. Hawking, S. (2016). The best or worst thing to happen to humanity. Speech presented at the launch of the Leverhulme Centre for the Future of Intelligence. Cambridge: University of Cambridge.

4. Nayler, R. (2023). AI and the rise of mediocrity. *Time*. https://time.com/6337835/ai-mediocrity-essay/

5. https://www.statista.com/statistics/433871/daily-social-media-usage-worldwide/ (accessed 24 September 2024).

6. Go-Globe (2012). How people spend their time online [Infographic]. https://www.go-globe.com/how-people-spend-their-time-online-infographic/#:~:text=92%25%20of%20Internet%20users%20have,81%25%20for%20getting%20weather%20information (accessed 17 July 2024).

7. Li, Y.-Y., Sun, Y. and Meng, S.-Q. et al. (2021). Internet addiction increases in the general population during COVID-19: Evidence from China. *The American Journal on Addictions* 30 (4): 389–397. doi: 10.1111/ajad.13156

8. Evans, J.A. (2008). Electronic Publication and the narrowing of science and scholarship. *Science* 321 (5887): 395–399. doi:10.1126/science.1150473

9. Ahmad, S.F., Han, H. and Alam, M.M. et al. (2023). Impact of artificial intelligence on human loss in decision making, laziness and safety in education. *Humanities and Social Sciences Communications* 10 (1): 311. https://doi.org/10.1057/s41599-023-01787-8

10. https://www.bcg.com/publications/2023/how-people-create-and-destroy-value-with-gen-ai (accessed 25 September 2024).

12

Curiosity and Corporate Culture

> "We keep moving forward, opening new doors, and doing new things, because we're curious and curiosity keeps leading us down new paths."
>
> Walt Disney

Trigger Question: how curious did you feel at work last week?

Curiosity is the engine of growth in today's world. It's what moves us forward, generates new ideas, and helps us and the world around us to evolve. Curiosity helps us challenge the status quo, moves us from entropy to evolution, and enables us to continue to test, learn, experiment, and grow. It's also at the heart of business success, with research suggesting it is the secret ingredient to successful, happier, more creative, and more inclusive workplaces.

We have been documenting the many benefits of curiosity in the workplace in previous chapters. Curiosity helps us learn faster and better, deepens our relationships, makes us more ready to accept change, increases our creativity, and overall enhances success. By adopting strategies used to build strong workplace cultures, organizations can harness the power of curiosity to drive innovation, employee well-being, and, ultimately, success in the ever-changing world of work.

In today's rapidly evolving business landscape, organizational culture has emerged as a critical factor in a company's success and is an area of growing importance for leaders. Forward-looking organizations like Patagonia, Nike, Disney, GE, Merck, Novartis, and Dell are increasingly adopting curiosity as a corporate value.

There are a growing number of companies that have embraced curiosity as a key tenet of their corporate culture. In this chapter, we delve into the intriguing relationship between curiosity and organizational culture and explore how curiosity can serve as a catalyst for success.

Defining Organizational Cultures

Organizational culture is an intangible yet powerful force that shapes how employees feel and behave at work, rather than a set of written rules. It encompasses shared beliefs, values, and norms, often summed up as "the way we do things around here". Recent research by Deloitte shows that 94% of executives and 88% of employees believe a strong corporate culture is vital for business success.[1] Companies with healthy cultures enjoy higher employee engagement and loyalty rates, elevated feelings of well-being, productivity, and overall success.

Furthermore, workplace culture significantly influences employee well-being, making it a top priority for organizations seeking success in today's competitive environment.

Curiosity-enhancing cultures are more likely to focus on innovation, experimentation, and diversity.

In working with many leadership teams over the last years, I find that risk-averse mature organizations often struggle to embrace curiosity, regardless of whether the leadership claims to value it. In contrast, start-ups tend to be more open to learning from failure, more curious about customers and products, and more exploration minded. My research has found that start-ups are four times more open to learning from failure compared to scale-up or mature organizations.

However, it does not have to be this way. A striking example is Disney+, an established company that has thrived and even overtaken its start-up rival Netflix. An important trait for such companies is creating psychological safety for employees to be bold, experiment, and take risks. This case proves that mature organizations can also overcome the pull towards conformity, invite curiosity, and be successful. Giving permission to do so, becoming aware of drivers and barriers and finally taking intentional actions are at the heart of successful curious companies.

Curiosity as a Catalyst for Success and Change

There's a compelling overlap between strong workplace cultures and organizations that value curiosity. Research has shown that curiosity-enabling cultures see greater levels of employee well-being, productivity, and innovation.

Curiosity also plays a pivotal role in driving organizational transformation and culture change. How does this work?

Most change initiatives in companies are often perceived as "Kotter style events". Dr John Kotter is the guru of change management. He created a system for tackling corporate transformations and designed an eight-step process for managing change initiatives. I personally have been part of multiple large-scale global projects where his methodology was followed like clockwork. What surprised me each time was that the approach was mechanical: an artificial urgency was created based on flawed assumptions. The story line of the change initiatives I witnessed was that unless we change we become irrelevant or lose our position. Senior management was the sponsor and multiple management layers had to be brought on board. Countless hours were spent on reviewing, and everybody involved needed to be trained by full-time change professionals, or people were hand-picked by their managers (versus being self-volunteered). The envisaged solution was always something that was needed to replace the old solution. External consultants told us how to go about this. It is no wonder that only a small percentage of change initiatives are claimed to have succeeded.

This same situation can be seen to occur when doctors stress to patients that they must change their diets, start exercising, stop bad habits, etc. or they will suffer serious, even life-threatening, consequences. Even in such life-threatening situations, not all patients follow their doctor's advice and make life changes.[2]

Journalist Dinah Wisenberg Bin reports in a well-researched article titled "Why Don't Patients Follow Their Doctors' Advice?" that 20–30% of prescriptions for chronic health conditions are never filled, and about half of the remaining prescriptions are not taken as directed. As much as we believe that appealing to "Damocles" moments is the best way to convince people to change their behaviour, this is not always the case.

A *Harvard Business Review* article shares an alternative approach to the one suggested by John Kotter. The CEO from a Brazilian company wanted to use a different approach for a change he had in mind. Instead of hiring consultants, creating a separate change team, committees of leaders, forming a two-year transformation plan, and focusing on the "we need to change, or else ..." narrative in addressing the required change, he decided to go grassroots and put out a "wanted" advert around the company. People who were drawn to the project could call the number on the ad. Unbeknownst to them, they called the personal phone of the CEO. The CEO brought these self-selected volunteers together and empowered them to figure out a new path for the company.[3]

The message is this: fear does not motivate people to make change. People change because they are energized about the future, when they see evidence close to them that things work, when they can experiment, when they have enough information to make up their own mind. Interestingly, all these points are hallmarks of curiosity. Change can be organic, it does not have to be highly structured. Listen for the right energy in your organization and bring the right positive deviants together. Give permission to the group to make things happen and let them follow their own energy.

Change management can be challenging, as humans tend to resist change and prefer the status quo. Curiosity, on the other hand, encourages us to view change as an opportunity for exploration and experimentation. Instead of conventional transformation programmes, organizations could adopt "curiosity programmes" to actively engage employees in creating the desired culture. A number of companies I worked with changed the narrative of "transformation and change" into one of "curiosity" and saw increased acceptance. In these companies, while "change" was perceived as something management had decided, "curiosity" was welcomed as an empowering invitation for people to get curious about the changes and adopt them into their routines.

Curiosity as a Corporate Value

Increasingly companies espouse curiosity as a value. It is sometimes directly expressed as "curiosity" or indirectly referenced as, for example, "not bound by convention", "pioneering", "always day one", "growing together", and so on.

In Chapter 3, when we discussed the power of permission, we shared some examples of companies who had adopted curiosity as a corporate value. Organizations who select curiosity as a value understand four essential dimensions.

- That curiosity is a concept that surpasses the individual realm and strongly influences a collective mindset. The firm has a role to play in creating the right environment for curiosity and in defining what is meant by the concept of curiosity.

- They recognize that, due to the ever-increasing speed of change and information in today's business landscape, curiosity is assumed to be even more critical than it has been in the past and that focusing on it is imperative to secure future success.

- That embracing curiosity at the level of the corporate values is an overt statement to all stakeholders that this concept is embraced, nurtured, and rewarded.

- That the company's leadership team has internalized the many benefits of unleashing curiosity at work.

Selecting and communicating values is a crucial first step. It announces in no uncertain terms that there is permission to act. Selection and communication are, however, only the first steps. It is common knowledge that many companies are struggling to operationalize their values. Estimates suggest that only a minority of companies have successfully integrated their values into their day-to-day operations. Also, according to research done by Fond, only about one in ten HR leaders believe that 80% or more of their employees are able to recite their company values.[4] What is crucial is for leadership to move beyond crafting strong values and make them a lived reality within the organization.

I am a believer in the power of words. Words hold immense power and translate chosen corporate values into actions. I have been part of several initiatives with companies to construct meaning around the concept of "curiosity". What do we mean by "curiosity" in our context, what do we consider good versus bad curiosity?

In working with companies, I find that the concept of curiosity is often not well defined, communicated, and operationalized across the organization, which results in confusion. Furthermore, curiosity carries regional negative connotations, such as "curiosity killed the cat" in English or "curiosity is the first step to Hell" in the Polish language. Making sure a clear definition is in place avoids misinterpretations.

A case of a global Italian foods company proves this point. The company initially espoused curiosity as one of its core values when it was founded. However, as professional managers took over the company's reins 50 years later, they adopted a more risk-averse and efficiency-based strategy that was at odds with the founders' vision. While the company kept the curiosity value on the corporate PowerPoints, they had not updated the original connotations (entrepreneurship and risk taking) of the term. After a dedicated effort, a new definition of curiosity was created (curiosity in the service of diversity and customers).

Let's look at our trigger question from this chapter. Since 2023, I have been asking a simple question in my curiosity diagnostics: how curious did you feel at work last week? Of all the companies I have surveyed with this question, the highest score been 75%, the lowest 46%. Digging deeper into these scores, senior executives and individual contributor professionals have a greater tendency to assign higher values to this question than middle level managers. In a recent company I worked with, middle managers rated themselves at 29% on this question. This is also the group that reports having the least time to be curious at work. If you want to be serious about embracing curiosity, a good place to start is with a focus on middle management.

Operationalizing Curiosity into Processes and Practices

Creating clarity on values is key. We can think about every moment in an employee's lifecycle and how to embed core values and behaviours, or how curiosity drives innovation, either with or without the customer present. Many organizations have started to operationalize curiosity as a behaviour:

- Hiring for Curiosity: Companies like Merck have made curiosity a central element in their recruitment process and recruitment branding, actively seeking individuals who are curious and open to exploring new ideas and solutions.[5] The company also trains their recruitment teams in the different aspects of curiosity.

- Continuous Learning Focus: Novartis, a global healthcare company, encourages employees to spend 5% of their time or 100 hours a year developing their curiosity. They host webinars, fund holistic training, and inspire their employees through curiosity-based events.

- Offering a Safe Space to Ask Difficult Questions: Ed Catmull, co-founder of Pixar, highlights the significance of creating a secure environment for open discussions and feedback. Pixar employs "Braintrust" meetings, where team members convene to offer frank feedback on projects without hierarchical constraints. This approach allows for the free exchange of ideas and collaborative exploration of creative solutions.

Moreover, Pixar hosts "Notes Day", an event where normal work activities are halted, and employees from all levels participate in brainstorming sessions to tackle various challenges. To ensure candidness, managers are excluded from these sessions. This practice fosters an atmosphere where everyone feels their input is valued and heard. These initiatives are integral to Pixar's strategy of promoting transparency, encouraging risk-taking, and supporting continuous learning, which are vital for sustaining their creative excellence and innovation.

- Rewarding Curiosity: Some companies actively reward and recognize employees who demonstrate curiosity by providing incentives, awards, or recognition programmes. DHL Global Forwarding hosts an annual Employee Appreciation Week with themes that celebrate diversity, inclusion, and innovation. The company also has an Employee of the Quarter/Year programme to recognize outstanding team members who contribute innovative ideas and demonstrate a curious mindset.[6]

- Job Rotation: Research by the Curiosity Institute and others has shown that after an initial "honeymoon" period, the curiosity of new employees goes down. Job rotation is an excellent method to ensure that employees remain fresh in their jobs. The food company PepsiCo went one step further, they also created a project marketplace inside the organization, where they invite part time and temporary support from colleagues from other departments, for example for four hours for four weeks, for internal applicants.

- Encouraging Employees to Spend Time in Different Environments: Great Ormand Street Hospital in London experienced significant numbers of casualties when transferring patients from the operating room to recovery. Physicians found inspiration after watching a Formula One racing team's efficiency in quickly servicing their cars. The race team was invited to view the hospital's transfer procedures and make observations based on their processes. The team's input helped the hospital dramatically reduce errors.[7]

- Celebrating Failure: Some organizations, like Ben and Jerry's, embrace the concept of celebrating failure. They are willing to let go of what is no longer successful and even conduct business funerals to mark the end of products or initiatives that didn't work. They even have a "flavour graveyard".[8]

  The software company Intuit celebrates failures in official "failure parties".[9] These approaches not only encourage curiosity and experimentation, but also create a culture that is open to taking risks.

- Complementing Organizational Values with Team Values: Another way to operationalize curiosity is to encourage teams to translate the company's values into team values. This allows for a more customized and empowered implementation of the values at the team level. By aligning team values with company values, organizations can ensure that these values are not just words but are reflected in the everyday actions and decisions made at the team level.

For an organization to truly live its values and embedded behaviours across its operations, it may not always feel comfortable. Take curiosity, for example. With more people asking difficult questions, challenging the status quo, reflecting on their behaviour, and being curious about people and solutions, it's likely that there will be uncomfortable moments. In the short term, this may create tension that the organization or the team is not accustomed to.

Curiosity Hacks for Companies

Curiosity is a team sport. Curious individuals need curious organizations to thrive. Organizations have a responsibility to help their employees develop their curiosity. Here are some strategies to cultivate a culture of curiosity:

- Create Permission for Curiosity: Communicate that curiosity is an appreciated value for the organization, with a clear definition of what it means. Companies that embed curiosity in their corporate values give permission at the highest level to explore, experiment, suggest improvements, and invite new product ideas.

(continued)

(*continued*)

- Review Current Processes and Practices: Leadership teams should audit their core and non-core processes through the lens of curiosity, such as customer interfaces, innovation pipelines, and people processes.

- Role Modelling: Senior executives should exhibit curiosity, be open to sharing both the good and the bad, maintain a learning mindset when interacting with employees, and invite positive dissent at crucial organizational junctures.

- Encourage Experimentation: Ensure time and space are available for experimentation. For example, organize company hackathons to invite employees to contribute their thoughts and ideas.

- Celebrate Failures: Ensure that a first-time mistake is seen as a learning opportunity, not a career-limiting action. For instance, Intuit gives a special award for the Best Failure and holds "failure parties" to celebrate learning opportunities.

- Embed Curiosity in HR Processes: Make curiosity an integral part of recruitment, promotion, rewards, learning and development, and diversity and inclusion strategies.

- Include Curiosity in Leadership Development: Create training for all employees, especially leaders, to reflect on curiosity and learn hacks to get better at it. Not all employees will be keen to stick their necks out at first; many will need reassurance and new skills to help them on their curiosity journey.

- Measure Curiosity: Baseline both individual curiosity as well as the organizational aspects of curiosity to celebrate strengths and prioritize areas for improvement. Create KPIs in areas you want to measure individual, team, or organizational curiosity.

In any organization, some individuals may find it challenging to live up to the organization's values and behaviours, and addressing this issue is a necessary challenge for leaders. For sustainable growth, discomfort is often unavoidable, especially in fast-changing environments. Companies cannot afford to remain stagnant or maintain the status quo. Exploring the future, even in uncertain times, is a vital part of the game.

Ditto for exploring the future of our planet, which we will discuss in the next chapter. We'll see that curiosity is a wonderful antidote to our current ecological crisis on several fronts. Are you interested in exploring the societal implication of curiosity for our planet?

Questions for Reflection

- How curious did you feel at work last week? What factors contributed to your level of curiosity?
- How does your current workplace culture support or hinder curiosity and innovation?
- What systems or practices does your organization have in place to promote continuous learning and curiosity among employees?
- How well does your organization translate its values, including curiosity, into daily operations

and behaviours? What are some areas for improvement?

- What specific initiatives or programmes could your organization implement to foster a culture of curiosity and experimentation?

Notes

1. https://www2.deloitte.com/content/dam/Deloitte/global/Documents/About-Deloitte/gx-core-beliefs-and-culture.pdf
2. Brin, D.W. (2017). *Why Don't Patients Follow Their Doctors' Advice?* Washington: AAMC. https://www.aamc.org/news/why-don-t-patients-follow-their-doctors-advice
3. Ricardo, S. (2014). How We Went Boss-Free. *Harvard Business Review* 92 (11): 112–121.
4. https://www.fond.co/blog/new-data-company-core-values/
5. https://www.randstad.com/workforce-insights/employer-branding/case-study-employer-branding-merck/ (accessed 25 September 2024).
6. https://group.dhl.com/en/media-relations/press-releases/2024/dhl-express-in-first-place-among-the-worlds-best-workplaces.html?utm_source=chatgpt.com (accessed 25 September 2024).
7. Sower, V.E., Duffy J.A. and Kohers, G. (2008). Great Ormond Street Hospital for Children: Ferrari's Formula One Handovers and Handovers from Surgery to Intensive Care. https://asq.org/quality-resources/articles/case-studies/great-ormond-street-hospital-for-children-ferraris-formula-one-handovers-and-handovers-from-surgery-to-intensive-

care?id=fbc699af11d04980ade06f409a5d6f98&utm (accessed August 2024)

8. https://www.benjerry.com/whats-new/2015/flavor-grave%20yard-depinted (accessed 25 September 2024).

9. https://www.happy.co.uk/blogs/8-companies-that-celebrate-mistakes/ (accessed 25 September 2024).

13

Curiosity and the Planet

"I am always astonished by a forest. It makes me
realize that the fantasy of nature is much larger
than my own fantasy. I still have things to learn."

Gunther Grass

**Trigger Question: if you could weigh all the wild ani-
mals in the sea and on land, how much would wild
animals weigh compared to all domesticated animals?**

When astronauts view the blue marble called
Earth from space, they are experiencing what
they call "the great overview". They have a balcony
moment very few of us will ever experience when
they are looking down upon us. Actually, there is no
"us" that they see. They see a blue world with no
borders and no humans. I imagine they are in awe of
the fragile beauty in front of their eyes.

Curiosity transcends the boundaries of personal
and professional spheres. Its potential to drive sustainable practices and contribute to a more environmen-
tally conscious world is a topic worthy of comprehensive
exploration. The only thing we need to do is to stop
and look at our own situation, like astronauts do.

In this chapter, we go broad. It is a chapter of
hope. A fragile hope. We'll discuss how the environmental landscape of our planet is rife with challenges, from the ominous spectre of climate change
to the insidious spread of pollution and the loom-
ing threat of resource depletion. As we confront
these formidable issues, it becomes increasingly

evident that curiosity, with its intrinsic qualities of questioning the status quo and seeking new answers, is a crucial driving force propelling us towards exciting new sustainable solutions. At the same time, curiosity also invites us to change some of our disruptive behaviour.

A Natural Connection We Have Forgotten

In contrast to astronauts, down here on Earth we can be oblivious to the magic splendour we are part of. Have we forgotten that we are part of nature? Since the seventeenth century or so, we've thought of ourselves as being separate from nature. We have to go the local park to feel a connection with nature, not realizing that our bodies are 100% part of nature, needing sustenance and water. The COVID-19 pandemic has reminded us that we are indeed part of nature. Even more, that tampering with external environments, food sources, and fragile ecosystems, all in the name of progress, is at best a hit and miss exercise.

Sometimes our experiments in environmental improvement work, sometimes they blow up in our faces. There are lots of wonderful examples of promising initiatives, however. The challenge is that these are still more the minority than mainstream. Why? Because safeguarding the planet is such a big and complex question that many people and organizations prefer the cosy environment of conformity over curiosity. It is easier to practise strategic ignorance over asking clarifying questions. Even when we are confronted with overwhelming evidence that our Earth is sputtering, we cling to stories about why the status quo is not that bad. Sometimes such strategic ignorance comes from a place of self-preservation: to retain a level of sanity through not knowing the potential issues facing us, to justify keeping the status quo or because we have other things to worry about.

At the same time, there is a growing understanding that the planet is worth saving. Kids are being taught a rekindled love of nature in schools, youngsters are marching the streets led by modern-day heroes like Greta Thunberg. The drivers of change are people under 30 and over 70—people without mortgages—trying to convince the other group— the people with economic and political power—to make the right decisions. Momentum is growing, yet it is not big enough to claim victory. We know from behavioural science that for any new idea to see the light of day, it needs about 25% of the group to buy in in order to create a shift.[1]

Some People Just Do It and Show the Way

An Apple ad campaign titled "Here's to the crazy ones" celebrated such curious creatives as Einstein,

Gandhi, Amelia Earhart, Mohammad Ali, Richard Branson, Bertrand Russell, and others:

> Here's to the crazy ones.
> The misfits.
> The rebels.
> The troublemakers.
> The round pegs in the square holes.
> The ones who see things differently.
> They're not fond of rules.
> And they have no respect for the status quo.
> You can praise them, disagree with them, quote them, disbelieve them, glorify or vilify them.
> About the only thing you can't do is ignore them.
> Because they change things.
> They invent. They imagine. They heal.
> They explore. They create. They inspire.
> They push the human race forward.

Phil Asmundson is another individual who challenges the status quo and shows the way.

He was just returning from a trip to his Malbec vineyard in Argentina and was looking over his land in southern Arizona. His old Dell computer was buzzing on his table in his shack. A passionate winemaker, he was grateful for so many things. That his wife had bought him his first vineyard when he retired from his demanding job as Chairman of Deloitte and that he had won prizes in blind taste tests in France with his wine. Most of all he was pleased that he had been able to make wine in an area just 20 miles from the Mexican border, an area in Arizona known for its climate challenges: lack of water, dry air, cold winters, and everything else. Not only had he made quality wine better than French wines, but he had done so with a 96% reduction in the use of insecticides when compared to his fellow winemakers.

His Dell computer sounded a beep and Phil looked down at it with a smile. One of the many sensors on his property hooked up to his computer beeped. This sensor is a small open box with no walls and only a top and bottom held together by four pillars, one at each corner. There's a little memory chip placed on the bottom together with a little piezo electric microphone. The memory chip stores a database of the frequency of the wing beats of thousands of insects, both harmless and harmful insects. If an insect with a wing beat of 180 hertz flies through the device, it recognizes it as a house fly, but if an insect with a wing beat of say 170 hertz flies through it, it knows that it is a potentially harmful insect known as a thrip. If two of these insects fly through it, it sends a signal to the Dell computer that he might have a potential problem and might have to pump a little insecticide just to that region of the vineyard.

This is only one of the many types of devices he has installed. Some devices measure sunshine intensity, others shadow, and yet another measures moisture in the soil. This last looks like a metal pipe about a metre long (about three feet) pounded into the ground. It has little holes about every 2 centimetres (inch). A little wireless transmission unit on top of the pipe measures soil water content. In traditional farming, farmers water their plants by flooding the field. A large percentage of that water is wasted as it either does not reach its destination or evaporates in the heat of the sun. Here's what Phil does: these devices measure the water content of the soil and, as the water percolates down into the soil, when it reaches a certain depth the little transmission unit signals to stop watering and turns off the water supply to that part of the vineyard.

The most important part is a matter of unintended consequences. All of the data from all of these devices is aggregated in a little Dell computer: and Phil discovered something really interesting. Not only do these sensors measure where the water level is, but they also measure the depth at which the grapes actually drink. Some varieties drink at 50 centimetres, some at 30 centimetres, and some at 22 centimetres. So, what now happens is that all of these different regions of the vineyard are independently watered to exactly the depth that the plants need the water. He has reduced his water consumption in the Arizona desert by 88%.

There are a couple of lessons to learn from Phil's story. It takes a fresh pair of eyes to make a difference.

Giving permission to new ways of doing things is easier when we adopt a beginner's mindset. Technology and data can create new opportunities. Keeping curiosity alive and paying attention to unintended consequences can unlock new insights and knowledge.

Vertical Farming

Another equally inspiring and successful example is the concept of vertical farming, which has gained traction recently in the aftermath of COVID-19. One of the challenges that has occurred in the post COVID-19 world is that we have large numbers of office buildings in central business districts in the downtown areas of cities that are vacant because people never came back to work. What is starting to happen is that modern farmers are approaching the landlords of these buildings with the promise of renting them. The only condition is that they want all indoor floors removed. Let's take an example of a 10-storey building. They then go in and build shelves where vegetables are grown. Every metre and a half from the ground floor up to the ceiling 10 floors higher they stack shelves above each other.

To provide the necessary nutrients to the plants they have a choice between traditional soil crop farming or other more modern technologies, such as hydroponics where the roots are simply sitting in water. Another technique is called aeroponics where the roots are in the air but they get sprayed with a nutrient solution. Then there's something called *aquaponics*. Aquaponics is fascinating: it's two tanks one on top of another. The top one has nutrient solution in it and the plants are in it. The tank below is filled with water and fish. The fish are fed and when they poop it creates nitrites, which is what plants need to eat. So the water from the fish tank is pumped up into the plants, the plants pull the nitrates out as food, thus cleaning the water, which then is pumped back into the fish tank, making a complete and closed cycle.

The success of such vertical farming projects has been positive indeed. For a 10-storey building, there is a multiplication factor of 50 of available space to grow crops. So, if your building has available space of say 50 by 50 metres (2,500 square metres), the arable space is 125,000 square metres. Further, food can be grown locally, can be managed optimally, multiple crops can be grown per year (and crops can vary across shelves), food is fresher to the consumer, and the practice creates local jobs.

Why this is so important is because it solves some of the big problems of traditional food production and distribution, such as water shortages, climate change influencing crop growing, transportation and storage costs, dependencies on pesticides and herbicides, and overall food quality.

These sustainable vertical farms allow local production. Instead of food production in only some select parts of the world (e.g., California, Israel, or Argentina) and then shipping to the rest of the world, in vertical farming, food is produced and distributed locally, thereby eliminating expensive transportation costs and decreasing harvest-to-plate time. Local farmers, local supply chains, and the local economy all benefit. Stephen Shepard, who has researched vertical farming extensively and introduced me to the concept, shared with me that "the biggest advantage is that the current model is simply not sustainable anymore. Water is drying up in California. Vertical farming has a powerful and compelling case."

I resonated immediately with Stephen's thoughts. A part time organic farmer myself on a small plot of 6 hectares (12 acres), I realized the upside and potential.

There are lots of examples like these, and many individuals, companies, and governments are leading the way. But we are not there yet. We have not yet reached the critical mass of supporters for the tipping point towards a net zero society. Saving the planet will remain a challenge for years and generations to come. Multiple forces are pulling us in the opposite direction. What is needed right now is more commitment by more people to push for change. Without that commitment, we could miss our chance to turn things around. We are now in a situation that's exemplified by this Cherokee story: "An old Cherokee is teaching his grandson about life. A fight is going on inside me", he said to the boy.

"It is a terrible fight and it is between two wolves. One is evil—he is anger, envy, sorrow, regret, greed, arrogance, self-pity, guilt, resentment, inferiority, lies, false pride, superiority, and ego." He continued, "The other is good—he is joy, peace, love, hope, serenity, humility, kindness, benevolence, empathy, generosity, truth, compassion, and faith. The same fight is going on inside you—and inside every other person, too."

The grandson thought about it for a minute and then asked his grandfather, "Which wolf will win?"

The old Cherokee simply replied, "The one you feed."

The question is: which wolf are we feeding when it comes to the planet? The one that saves it or the one that ignores the fact that something is about to happen?

Giving in to Permission

Behaviour change is hard: 99% of children follow not only their parents' religion, but perhaps surprisingly their diet. Ample evidence indicates that eating less meat is not only good for your health, it is also good for the planet. To produce one kilogram of beef requires a staggering 2,400 litres of water. In my native Belgium, over 90% of the agricultural land is used to either grow livestock feed or for grazing. If we were to eat less meat, farmers could grow vegetables for humans. If we eat less meat, there would be less creation of methane, which is a significant contributor to global warming.

Remember the question we asked in the beginning of the chapter? The Weizmann Institute of Science has calculated that the weight of all animals in the wild, from huge whales to small ants, collectively weighs about 60 million tons. Are you curious about how many animals we have running around to feed us humans? There are more than 10 times as many domesticated animals: cows, pigs, sheep, and chickens are reared to give us our daily hamburger, bacon, or chicken wings: a staggering 630 million tons in total.[2] When I first saw this data, it set me thinking about what I could do to mitigate the problems this situation is causing. Permission and change, however small, starts with me.

When my daughter started fighting to save the planet in her teens and joined national youth committees, I was proud of her. When I saw her become burned out because of the lip service politicians and industry paid to the problem, I became frustrated. I learned later that there is even a clinical term for what she was going through: eco-anxiety. The American Psychology Association (APA) describes eco-anxiety as "the chronic fear of environmental cataclysm that comes from observing the seemingly irrevocable impact of climate change and the associated concern for one's future and that of next generations".

The frustration I felt observing my daughter's burnout gave me energy to do something about the issue at my level. I bought land, became a part time organic farmer, and became a beekeeper. I have planted now over 200 fruit and nut trees, close to 1,000 berry plants and bushes, and have surrounded the property with an insect-friendly hedge. I am starting a community initiative to grow fully organic vegetables and have committed 25% of all revenues from my consulting work to be reinvested in nature projects.

Taking Small Positive Steps

Government and industry have their role to play. Each of us can also play a much bigger role. One thing we have not discussed in this chapter is how we can change our behaviour. In the entire planet discussion, there is one line of thinking that suggests technology holds the keys to a better future. Technology definitely has a huge role to play, yet alone cannot save the world. There is another side of the coin we easily forget: we need to change our habits and behaviours.

I reduced my air travel by 90%. A good thing that came out of the changes ushered in during COVID-19 was that companies got used to online meetings. The majority of my work, my keynotes and consulting work with companies, I do online. If I need to do a gig in London or Spain, I happily take a 3 or 10 hour train ride. Actually, I have found that these train rides are much more relaxing than air travel and give me better quality thinking time. My wife and I are also increasingly buying locally sourced products: over the last three years we have ordered our books via local bookstores instead of giving the business to global online retailers. When we go for a coffee outside, we choose local players over big chains.

What these small steps have in common is that they are hugely empowering. They give us wings. Realizing that sticking with the status quo won't get us anywhere we want to be. Conformity will surely lead us to a lesser place. With the right permission, awareness, and intentionality, we might turn things around. Individual intentionality and action are important. In communities around the world, hundreds of thousands of people are becoming more knowledgeable every day and are taking small and big steps. Steps of hope. In increasing numbers, small and large experiments are seeing the light of day, every day.

The very notion of success—individual success as well as organizational success—is being metamorphosed into something new. New thinking about success will bring curiosity further into mainstream thinking; it will also transform us as individuals, organizations, and even societies. This will be the focus for our concluding summary chapter. Are you curious still?

Questions for Reflection

- How can giving permission, awareness, and intentionality in daily life lead to a more sustainable future? What are the potential implications for your business?

- How can fresh perspectives and a beginner's mindset, as exemplified by Phil, lead to significant environmental advancements?
- How does viewing Earth from space change our perspective on environmental issues and our connection to nature?
- How can individual lifestyle changes, such as reducing air travel and supporting local businesses, contribute to environmental conservation?
- What actions can you take as an organization to drive sustainable practices in your organization and community?

Notes

1. Kashdan, T.B. (2022). *The Art of Insubordination: How to Dissent and Defy Effectively*. New York: Avery.
2. Milo, R., Greenspoon, L., and Moran, U. et al. (2023). The global biomass of wild mammals. *Proceedings of the National Academy of Sciences* 120 (10): e2204892120. https://doi.org/10.1073/pnas.2204892120

14

Putting It All Together

"Two roads diverged in a wood, and I—I took the one less traveled by, And that has made all the difference."

Robert Frost, Poet

"To laugh often and much; to win the respect of intelligent people and the affection of children; to earn the appreciation of honest critics and endure the betrayal of false friends; to appreciate beauty; to find the best in others; to leave the world a bit better, whether by a healthy child, a garden patch or a redeemed social condition; to know even one life has breathed easier because you have lived. This is to have succeeded."

Ralph Waldo Emerson, Author

Trigger Question: what is your next step?

We have been exploring curiosity: what it is, what it does, and how it works. It is no coincidence that it is being named as the meta skill for the twenty-first century, as without it, we will not be able to face the challenges that are in front of us.

Curiosity is the lubricant of the twenty-first century. It is the meta skill leading to divergent thinking, new opportunities, deeper empathy, and openness. It helps us to ask deeper and better questions and prepares us for possibilities.

Unlike its past negative connotation, curiosity is nowadays rightfully celebrated as a strength and a positive force. From an evolutionary perspective, curiosity is crucial for species survival. It drives an agent to explore anything new, uncertain, complex, or ambiguous in their environment. This exploration can lead to rewards, such as discovering where to find new food, the medicinal value of plants, and attaining social status.

Curiosity makes people—and animals—sensitive to internal and external changes that could signal potential threats, injuries, or dangers. It is the precursor to creativity, fostering the design of new and useful contributions that are more likely to be valued, accepted, and protected. At a societal level, curiosity fuels economies, inspires paradigm-shifting inventions, and offers solutions to global crises.

Psychologically, people with higher levels of curiosity tend to achieve more and enjoy better health and well-being. They often experience greater vitality, meaning, and purpose in life, and overall satisfaction.[1] Curious professionals are more likely to become successful entrepreneurs with larger social and professional networks.

However, curiosity is challenging and energy consuming. The lure of conformity often discourages curiosity. Competing demands for our time and attention lead to unintended costs. Metabolically, the brain consumes significant energy to process new information. Socially, those who constantly seek novelty may be perceived as eccentric or disruptive. Psychologically, the relentless pursuit of novelty can be mentally exhausting.

Curiosity is often seen as the enjoyable pursuit of new knowledge, but it comes in more than one form. There is interest-type curiosity and deprivation-type curiosity, the latter being an uncomfortable urge to fill an information gap.[2] Both types have metabolic costs, as they involve orienting attention to new information, detecting gaps, and making sense of the object of curiosity.[3] Deprivation sensitivity carries additional burdens, such as a restless need to know and frustration triggered by a lack of information. I-type curiosity correlates positively with well-being; D-type curiosity, however, correlates negatively with it and can lead to burnout if its level remains high over time.

While curiosity is explicitly praised, there is often implicit bias against curious workers by bosses, possibly due to the perception that curious employees are more challenging to manage and tend to ask difficult questions.[4] Primary school teachers also show a similar dichotomy between valuing curiosity in theory and their treatment of students who ask many questions. They say they prefer curious pupils, yet their behaviour suggests they prefer to work with the lesser curious children.

When we delve into the complex nature of curiosity, a new world unfolds.

Follow some of the suggestions in this book, and you will become stronger, wiser, more open-minded. More interested in the world around you, more in sync with the people you work and live with and more in tune with your deeper self. If millions of us set aside some of our conformist thinking in favour of curiosity, we'll build safer, more prosperous, more dynamic, more futureproof, and more harmonious communities and enterprises.

The transformational power of curiosity is remarkable. It leads to the following.

- Better Decision-making: curious professionals and leaders gather more information and consider diverse perspectives before making choices.
- Sustainable Innovation: curiosity drives the exploration of new ideas and solutions.
- People Engagement: curious leaders create an environment where team members feel valued and empowered to share their thoughts.
- Greater Adaptability: curiosity helps to navigate change and uncertainty by remaining open to new inputs and adjusting course.

These attributes are true for individuals as well as systems.

Throughout this book, we have seen that curiosity gives wings to every individual who gives it permission, becomes aware of its drivers and barriers, and acts with intentionality. My own research at the Global Curiosity Institute has highlighted that professionals who embrace curiosity make more money and achieve faster career progression when compared to their less curious peers. Not only that, curious beings live longer. Researchers found that rats that pursue new experiences have a 25% longer life expectancy than those rats who don't explore.[5] This is also true for humans; in 1996, psychologists concluded a research project where they followed people between 60 and 86 years old over a five-year period. They showed that people who were more intellectually curious at the start of the study had a greater probability of living until the end of the study, regardless of whether they were smokers, had heart disease, or any other impairment.[6]

Curiosity works. We have seen that curious people have more intense and fulfilling social contacts. Curious individuals ask the very questions that make others feel important. They are genuinely interested rather than trying to come across as interesting when communicating with others.

As we saw in Chapter 6, curious professionals, especially those who are high on I-type (interest-type) curiosity, report a greater sense of psychological well-being.[7] It is not surprising that curiosity is one of the top five character strengths and is most strongly correlated to life satisfaction, work satisfaction, and the ability to lead a life of enjoyment and meaning.[8]

A Gallup global survey of more than 130,000 people found that the two factors with the strongest influence on how much pleasure a person experienced on a given day were: "being able to count on someone who can help" and "having experienced something new yesterday".[9]

Curious individuals are also more self-confident. Harvard psychologist Ellen Langer showed that curiosity has the capacity to change one's perception of anxiety into a more positive experience, thereby giving people more self-confidence. She demonstrated that when our focus shifts away from what makes us anxious to what interests us, we react with less inhibition and are more ready to lean in to our fears.[10]

Curious people are more likely to develop interests, hobbies, and passions. They are more eager to learn new things. Curiosity drives us to learn more about a topic. The additional knowledge we gain in the process further increases our ability to solve problems, ask deeper questions, and come up with more creative suggestions.

When people are curious, they remember more. Matthias Gruber and his colleagues ran a study in which test participants were checked to see how well they could remember the answers to 40 questions three weeks after an initial test. What was the result? When they got the answer wrong the first time, they were better able to remember the correct answer. Curiosity facilitates learning, and helps us to consolidate new information in our memory.[11]

There is magic to curiosity at the individual level.

When curiosity is embraced at the collective level of a community, a team, or an organization, even more magic happens. When groups tune in to curiosity, success is guaranteed.

I have been reflecting on the link between success and curiosity for many years. How we think about success is a rather recent concept that was born about 250 years ago.

The current concept of success was born at the dawn of period known as the Enlightenment. Its meaning is encapsulated well in the famous quote by Immanuel Kant: "Sapere Aude"—"Dare to know". This phrase of 1784 started a new era: the era of curiosity. As from that point in time, new values were embraced such as reason, progress, and exploration.

Individualism was also a new mantra which came to the fore, which meant that achievement and success were measured against this new dimension. It is not strange that curiosity was initially thought of as an individual trait and success was primarily linked to individual agency. Success was about reaching individual goals. Once reached, people reaped the rewards. The self-help movement and gurus have been beating the drum that success is ultimately measured in material goods. If I reach the goals I set for myself, I will be able to make enough money to buy myself an enviable position in society. It is the American dream at its best: "I am the captain of my destiny."

In interviewing people for this book, I asked them about their definition of success. What quickly became clear was that the very concept of success is changing from one focused on reaching individual goals towards one with a clearly social tone. Of the more than 30 people I interviewed for this book, all the people I spoke to were more expansive in their definition: to them success has an explicit social dimension. More specifically: success is defined as how much value I add to people around me. Success is only success when it is inclusive.

I shared Ralph Waldo Emerson's definition of success at the beginning of this chapter. It emphasizes personal fulfilment, positive influence, and inner peace rather than conventional measures of success like wealth and status.

The main elements of Emerson's definition of success are as follows.

- Laughter and Joy: Finding happiness and spreading joy is a cornerstone of success. Being able to laugh often and find humour in life is essential.

- Respect and Affection: Earning the respect of intelligent people and the affection of children signifies a life well-lived, marked by integrity and kindness.

- Appreciation and Endurance: Valuing honest criticism and enduring betrayals with grace highlights the importance of resilience and humility.

- Appreciation of Beauty: Recognizing and appreciating beauty in the world, whether in nature, art, or people, enriches life.

- Finding the Best in Others: Seeing and nurturing the good in others fosters positive relationships and community.

- Leaving a Positive Impact: Making the world a better place, through small or significant actions.

- Making a Difference: Knowing that your life has positively impacted someone else, even in a small way, is a profound measure of success.

Emerson's holistic and humanistic approach to success focuses on personal growth, meaningful connections, and contributing to the well-being of others. It emphasizes that true success is about living a life of purpose and compassion.

Note that all these dimensions require curiosity in one shape or another. Permission, awareness, and intentionality across curiosity about the world, others, and oneself.

Being curious is a vital part of being human. I encourage you to create your own definition of curiosity and success. Make it as expansive as you can. Let me know what your next step is.

Notes

1. Kashdan, T.B. and Silvia, P.J. (2009). Curiosity and interest: the benefits of thriving on novelty and challenge. In: *The Oxford Handbook of Positive Psychology* 2e (eds. S. J. Lopez and C. R. Snyder), 366–374. Oxford: Oxford University Press. doi:10.1093/oxfordhb/978019 5187243.013.0034

2. Litman, J.A. (2005). Curiosity and the pleasures of learning: Wanting and liking new information. *Cognition and Emotion* 19 (6): 793–814. doi: 10.1080/02699930541 000101

3. Gruber, M.J. and Ranganath, C. (2019). How curiosity enhances hippocampus-dependent memory: The prediction, appraisal, curiosity, and exploration (PACE) framework. *Trends in Cognitive Sciences* 23 (12): 1014–1025. doi: 10.1016/j.tics.2019.10.003

4. Mueller, J.S., Melwani, S. and Goncalo, J.A. (2011). The bias against creativity: Why people desire but reject

creative ideas. *Psychological Science* 23 (1): 13–17. doi: 10.1177/0956797611421018

5. Cavigelli, S.A. and McClintock, M.K. (2003). Fear of novelty in infant rats predicts adult corticosterone dynamics and an early death. *Proceedings of the National Academy of Sciences of the United States of America* 100 (26): 16131–16136. doi: 10.1073/pnas.2535721100

6. Swan, G.E. and Carmelli, D. (1996). Curiosity and mortality in aging adults: A 5-year follow-up of 1,118 community-dwelling older men. *Psychology and Aging* 11 (3): 449–453. doi:10.1037/0882-7974.11.3.449

7. Litman, J.A. (2005). Curiosity and the pleasures of learning: Wanting and liking new information. *Cognition and Emotion*, 19 (6): 793–814. doi:10.1080/02699930541000176

8. Niemiec, R.M. (2013). https://www.psychologytoday.com/us/blog/what-matters-most/201311/the-5-happiness-strengths (accessed 25 September 2024).

9. Gallup. (2015). Global emotions report. https://www.gallup.com/services/184871/2015-global-emotions-report.aspx (accessed 25 September 2024).

10. Langer, E. (9 March 2005). Mindfulness and the positive impact of curiosity on reducing anxiety and increasing self-confidence. *Harvard Magazine*. https://hbr.org/2014/03/mindfulness-in-the-age-of-complexity.

11. Gruber, M.J., Gelman, B.D. and Ranganath, C. (2014). States of curiosity modulate hippocampus-dependent learning via the dopaminergic circuit. *Neuron* 84 (2): 486–496. https://doi.org/10.1016/j.neuron.2014.08.060 (accessed 31 October 2024).

Index